Class Construction

Class Construction

White Working-Class Student Identity in the New Millennium

Carrie Freie

LEXINGTON BOOKS

A division of
ROWMAN & LITTLEFIELD PUBLISHERS, INC.
Lanham • Boulder • New York • Toronto • Plymouth, UK

LEXINGTON BOOKS

A division of Rowman & Littlefield Publishers, Inc.
A wholly owned subsidiary of The Rowman & Littlefield Publishing Group, Inc.
4501 Forbes Boulevard, Suite 200
Lanham, MD 20706

Estover Road
Plymouth PL6 7PY
United Kingdom

British Library Cataloguing in Publication Information Available

Library of Congress Cataloging-in-Publication Data

Freie, Carrie, 1973–
  Class construction : white working-class student identity in the new millennium / Carrie
Freie.
     p. cm.
  Includes bibliographical references.
  ISBN-13: 978-0-7391-1547-3 (cloth : alk. paper)
  ISBN-10: 0-7391-1547-2 (cloth : alk. paper)
  1. Working class whites—Northeastern States. 2. High school students—Northeastern
States—Psychology. 3. High school students—Northeastern States—Attitudes. 4. High
school students—Social networks—Northeastern States. 5. Whites—Race identity—
Northeastern States 6. Gender identity—Northeastern States 7. Social networks—
Northeastern States 8. Northeastern States—Social conditions. 9. Northeastern States—
Economic conditions. I. Title.
  HD8083.N67F74 2007
  305.5'620974—dc22   2007007825

Printed in the United States of America
♾™ The paper used in this publication meets the minimum requirements of American
National Standard for Information Sciences—Permanence of Paper for Printed Library
Materials, ANSI/NISO Z39.48–1992

For Eric

Contents

Acknowledgments

This study could not have been done without the help of many. First and foremost I would like to thank the student participants who allowed me into their school and their lives. Without their generosity and openness this study would not have been possible.

In addition, thanks goes out to the administrators and teachers, though confidentiality keeps them from being named, who helped me to connect with the students and allowed me into their classrooms and lives.

Special thanks go to all those who have supported me from the beginning of this project, which began as my dissertation research. Lois Weis deserves special thanks for continually challenging me and pushing me to take my work to the next level. Her guidance was invaluable and I thank her for her dedication and inspiration. I would also like to thank Ruth Meyerowitz and Hank Bromley for their thoughtful comments and insightful perspectives.

I owe great thanks to colleagues who supported me in numerous ways, both by reading and commenting on my work, or simply offering to listen. Karyn St.George deserves special thanks for her honest comments on numerous drafts as well as helping to keep me on track. Thanks to Catie LaLonde for her feedback, friendship and catchy titles. Also thanks to Ramona SantaMaria, Michelle Meyers, and Catie; our lunches were an important time to reflect and I miss them!

To all of the people at University at Buffalo and Penn State Altoona who gave their support in countless ways, thank you. Scott DeWitt merits great thanks for his support and example.

I owe immeasurable thanks to all of my family and friends, more than I can express on this page. This work was made possible due to the encouragement I received from all of you. I would like to thank my husband Eric, whose support and encouragement helped to keep me focused, if not organized . . . though not for lack of trying. A special thanks to my parents and step-parents; my mother for her belief in me, and my father for his advice and example. I would also like to thank the Daums and the Witherells for keeping me grounded throughout this process. To all of my friends, both at the university and in other places, thank you for being there.

Chapter One

Introduction:
Welcome to River City

"The difficult thing to explain about how middle class kids get middle class jobs is why others let them. The difficult thing to explain about how working class kids get working class jobs is why they let themselves."

This is how Paul Willis opened *Learning to Labor* in 1977.[1] However, since early examinations in the sociology of working class life, what it means to be "working class" in the United States has changed a great deal. Mass consumerism, greater availability of college level education, lack of a cohesive class identity and racial and religious politics all swirl together to create new working-class identity for today's youth. The difficult thing to explain in the twenty-first century is not how working-class kids get working-class jobs but what working-class jobs look like. How is class conceptualized and in what ways is a cohesive class identity available or not available to today's youth? What roles do gender and racial dynamics play in the construction or obfuscation of class understanding in America? This ethnographic study aims to understand these issues through the lives of today's working-class youth and specifically through their experiences in school.

To set the scene for this work, it is necessary to touch on the changes in the American economy over the last decades. Living standards for working-class families in America have been declining since the 1970s.[2] Globalization in the 1980s and 1990s made it easier and cheaper for companies that once employed workers in the United States to produce goods in foreign countries. Many blue-collar production jobs moved or were lost, and more readily available service jobs that do not require special skills or post-secondary education are notoriously low paying and often unrewarding.[3] Supporting a family for most working-class and middle-class Americans now requires that all adults work outside of the home.[4] Much of the critical literature focusing on white working-class adolescents was done before and during deindustrialization, exploring traditional working-class culture during more prosperous times and then at the start of its decline.

The 1990s saw the creation of computer and internet-based jobs that usually required special skills and a college degree. Now the economic concern of the 2000s is the growing gap between the rich and the middle class and the movement of wealth upwards as the wages of the working and middle class begin to stagnate. Mantsios notes that, "[w]hile the real income of the top 1 percent of U.S. families skyrocketed by 59 percent during the economic boom of the late 1990s the middle fifth of the population grew only slightly and its share of income actually declined during this same period." Furthermore, "[s]ixty percent of the American population holds less

1

than 6 percent of the nation's wealth."[5] The idea of a "jobless recovery" represents this growing contrast between the rich and middle/working classes since an economic recovery based on stock market numbers has little meaning for the average worker. Despite what the media might portray, only about 40 percent of American households owned any stock in 2000. Ninety percent of American households (those with the lower incomes) own just 19 percent of the individually owned stocks, and many among this lower 90 percent owned no stock at all. In contrast, the wealthiest 1 percent of the population owns 38 percent of the nation's wealth, and the wealthiest 20 percent owns 83 percent of the total wealth which includes financial assets such as stocks. [6]

Those formerly employed in unionized factory jobs and their children are now looking to new sectors for employment in stretched economic times. As they look to find jobs in new niches and sometimes challenge traditional gender roles and family structures in pursuit of economic survival, these new working-class families are renegotiating what it means to be working class in the new millennium.[7]

For the purpose of this discussion I define class as one's relationship to the capitalist system, particularly the power one has over his or her own labor and the level of autonomy one has in his or her job as well as the lived social and cultural system one lives within. This is inclusive of, but not solely based on, cultural and behavioral habits.[8] Zweig and Reich both distinguish that the type of work one does is a significant defining factor of one's class. I find their contribution helpful for understanding the changing types of work and power relationships operating within the world of work post-deindustrialization. Zweig's definition focuses on power, "When I talk about class, I am talking about power. Power at work, and power in the larger society. Economic power, and also political and cultural power."[9] He defines the working class as one that has little or no authority at work or in general. Reich's analysis adds a further layer to the discussion of power and work. He defines two types of working-class jobs; "in-person service workers" are those who do their jobs face to face with clients and customers and "routine production service workers" are those who work in production and manufacturing. This distinction is based on job security: in-person service jobs cannot be exported as routine production service jobs can be and are moved elsewhere. Therefore, while in-person service jobs are often low-paying, such as fast food, retail, or secretarial jobs, they are based on providing a face-to-face service and consequently, not as likely to be moved overseas as routine-production service jobs.[10]

Though American society often defines the middle class as anyone but the extremely poor or extremely rich, a more nuanced way of approaching class, described above, leads to a very different breakdown of the numbers of working-class, middle-class, and upper-class people in the United States. Using a definition that takes into account one's autonomy and relationship to systems of power, the working class emerges as more than half of the workforce (62 percent according to Zweig's 2004 calculation). The middle class, those who have much more autonomy at work, are often someone else's boss and are often labeled as "professionals" or have jobs that require postsecondary education, skills, or training, make up 36 percent of the workforce.[11] The middle class also often have the cultural capital or the background, knowledge, disposition, and skills learned from families and social/educational institutions that allow them to access dominant institutions, communication styles, and forms of knowledge.[12] Reich defines upper middle-class people with highly professional jobs (those which require college and/or graduate degrees) as "symbolic analysts," or those who have a role in the construction of symbols and ideas in a way that impacts the lives of others.[13]

The cultural, knowledge-based, educational, and behavioral aspects of class and the working class in particular are also significant to this discussion. Anyon's examination of schooling for different classes of students points out how different communication styles, educational values, and types of knowledge are transmitted in schools. In this context, working-class students are encouraged to follow directions and behave in ways which are controlled by teachers or other outside forces.[14] Finn's work studies the ways this type of working-class education plays out in the lives of working-class students. His work highlights some of the unique aspects of working-class culture, such as the use of highly context-dependent forms of communication and a relationship to institutional power and authority, which is at the same time resistant, yet devoid of personal or group agency.[15] Weis's work, focusing on identity formation, explores group relationships and how these are experienced by the white working class—particularly the ways gender roles and gender identities are continually articulated and rearticulated, as are racial identities and relationships between groups. This re-working results in what Weis terms a "distinct class fraction" of the white working class, where gender roles, educational opportunities, the work one does, and racial relationships are renegotiated in new ways.[16]

The theoretical background for this study comes from literature exploring the reproduction of class, gender, and race as well as ethnographic studies done within schools. Much has been written about school as a site for the construction and negotiation of race, class, and gender identity. The literature reviewed in the next section explains how working-class adolescents create their identities based on their social and economic position in society and provides the background for the questions explored in this research.[17] The questions I will explore focus on the formation of social identity and how this is experienced and articulated by the high school students in this study.

Background

Literature has explored how working-class adolescents form class-based identities under the economic conditions of the 1970s, 1980s and early 1990s. I follow up by asking what happens in light of economic changes such as globalization and the transition of working-class jobs from unionized manufacturing jobs to non-unionized technological and white collar jobs. Facing different futures than their parents faced as high school students, I ask, in what ways do these white youth from working-class backgrounds construct their identities post-deindustrialization and against a backdrop of a changing economy and job market?

This ethnographic study explores class, racial, and gender identity construction among white working-class adolescents in high school. Focusing on the ways students' perceptions of their current and future classed, raced and gendered selves are negotiated within the context of the school, I explore the issues that are important to girls and boys. I also explore the school structure and the social structure within the school and how this structure lays the groundwork for how students relate to knowledge and how they explore and define their own classed and raced selves. The following are questions which have driven the research.

- How do white working-class youth in a large high school construct their identities with and against the social, academic and extracurricular areas of the school?
- What are the students' articulated relationships with other groups and agencies outside of the school, such as families, churches and places of employment?
- In what ways do these identities relate to perceptions of their future roles with respect to education, occupation, and family?

In addition to discussing these main questions that have driven my research, I will also explore how working-class culture is expressed in this new economic and cultural setting, in which unionized factory jobs are no longer readily available and in which traditional domestic expectations, of a man earning money while a woman stays home with the children, are no longer economically feasible for most working families. In *Class Reunion*, Weis discusses the ways in which traditional gender roles are being renegotiated in light of economic necessity. In order to maintain a stable household, both men and women pitch in to do whatever job needs to be done. This usually includes women working outside of the home, men helping with childcare and domestic duties, and might also include both men and women finding non-traditional employment; for example, a man working as a nurse, or a woman working in construction.[18] In light of these changes which have impacted the thirty-something generation, my study turns again to the adolescents and asks, how is "working class" now conceptualized by the youth? How do they understand and articulate their place in the world? What do they expect from their futures and how is this different from what their parents expected? And importantly, what is the role of the school, institutionally, socially, and culturally, in the production of identity, culture, and class?

Class Reproduction and Identity Formation

Willis's *Learning to Labor* is one of the first works to identify cultural reproduction as lived by youth.[19] Framed in an economic setting where working-class jobs are available to the young men, Willis discusses how the culture of the group of boys he calls "lads" perpetuates values, such as resistance to authority, independence, and worldliness, which ultimately lead the lads away from the school and into factory work. The "lads" define themselves relationally in opposition to gendered and racial "others" as well as in opposition to other groups of white students, mainly the group they refer to as the "ear 'oles" who they view as buying into the system of authority represented by the school. While the "ear 'oles" do well in school, the "lads" shun school success and reject school authority. The "lads" seek out adult jobs and find them in factories where the "shopfloor culture" parallels the anti-authority standpoint the "lads" established at school. At first, many of the lads find working on the shop floor and the accompanying financial rewards liberating, but ultimately Willis reveals this as reproduction of the working class.

While the "lads" experience "penetrations" or moments of critique in which they become aware of the reproductive nature of the system in which they take part, ultimately they perpetuate the cycle and recreate traditional working-class culture complete with its hierarchical family structure and subordinate economic position.

Willis's work situates its discussion around a historic conception of class that is widely acknowledged in British society. In other words, the term "working class" was one the lads used to identify themselves. In the United States, particularly today, one is much less likely to find a group of people self-identifying as working class. Instead, the term "middle class" seems to be a catchall, spanning categories that are arguably working class or upper class. As already noted, in this volume I use the term "working class" in an attempt to express a social and economic relationship to the larger system which is specifically sensitive to educational, social, and economic relationships. It is important to use the term "working class" in order to situate the relationship of this group firmly within an economic and educational sector which is less privileged than others identified as middle class. While I am not using the term in a way that solely focuses on one's relationship with the means of production, as traditional definitions might, I am committed to using the term as a way to keep the focus on a group positioning that is importantly different from a middle class or upper class one.

Work like Willis's initial research on class reproduction and the role of lived culture spurred discussions about what spaces and roles working-class youth might occupy in the deindustrializing economy of the 1980s. In this economy, factory jobs were not readily available or were disappearing as factories closed, downsized, or moved to locations outside of the United States.

For the purpose of this study, I define identity as the way one defines oneself within social networks and in relation to others. Importantly, identity is formed in contrast and in opposition to other groups. It is fluid and it is continually reformed and reshaped. Identity is a significant factor in determining what one envisions as an appropriate occupation, gender role, and behavior, as well as how one interacts with others and how one makes sense of the world around them. The works discussed here each focus on different aspects of identity formation.[20] Factors such as class, race, gender, and so on, emerge as significant in the identity development of students in the various environments. Though no one factor is more significant than another, these categories are neatly divided for purposes of discussion and analysis. However, the ways they work in actual life situations is often unpredictable, multifaceted, and intertwining. These categories, importantly, are not static but constantly being defined, redefined, explored, and negotiated. In my fieldwork and in the following discussion, each of these factors surfaces in different ways.

Continuing to explore the everyday lives of white working-class adolescents, Weis's *Working Class Without Work* presents working-class adolescents' perceptions of themselves and their futures as they are situated within a rapidly deindustrializing economy. She discusses how the youth envision their own futures in terms of education, jobs, marriage and family in the face of economic uncertainty. As the jobs in manufacturing disappear, the adolescents are forced to rethink their futures. Similar to Willis's "lads," the boys in *Working Class Without Work* define themselves as different from other racial groups and the other gender. Because of this, they see themselves as at odds with these other groups. African-Americans are seen as both a threat to "their" jobs and a threat to "their" (read: white) women. In addition, they adhere to traditional hierarchical roles with women, an idea their female cohorts do not generally share. The girls experience "moments of critique" in which they eschew these traditional gender roles and envision themselves pursuing education and careers and being able to provide for themselves. Like Willis, Weis's work focuses on group identities formed around economic relationships, though unlike Willis, Weis devotes attention to both male and female adolescents as they reflect on their lives.

Class Reunion is Weis's follow-up on *Working Class Without Work* in which she returns to interview some of the participants in the original volume.[21] In this new exploration, Weis theorizes the reshaping of the white working class as a "distinct class fraction." In order to survive economically and live what Weis terms "settled lives," traditional gender roles are being reworked, not so much through verbal articulations, but through lived experience. In these settled households, both men and women usually work outside of the home and contribute economically in order to maintain a comfortable lifestyle, and men take on domestic responsibilities. The higher education that, as girls, these women talked about has become a reality for many of them, though not without some struggle. Those who do not embrace a new gender dynamic Weis refers to as "hard living" people who often struggle economically and are unable to experience the stability the settled households enjoy. While gender roles are being reworked, racial boundaries are reinforced as both white men and women join together to solidify racial lines and protect their schools, neighborhoods and jobs from racial "others."

Class Reproduction and Hidden Curriculum

The mainstream concept of schooling views the educational system as a meritocracy. However, this view is profoundly at odds with the great inequalities within schools as well as the inequality of outcomes. Bowles and Gintis's *Schooling in Capitalist America* explains how economic reproduction works in America's schools.[22] Bowles and Gintis say that in a capitalist society, there must be those who work the jobs in each level of production. In order for the system to work, workers need to be prepared to act out their roles in the system. This is where the school system comes in, preparing workers to take on jobs similar to those their parents hold. Through the hidden curriculum, workers are taught the latent skills they will need to take on the jobs for which they are being prepared. Anyon more specifically elaborates on how hidden curriculum plays out at different socioeconomic levels.

Anyon's work on hidden curriculum analyzes interactions within a school, particularly the expectations of teachers and administrators that help to shape what and how students learn and what future work they are being prepared for.[23] Her study compares four schools in different socio-economic areas. She finds that although the schools share a formal curriculum, the hidden curriculum, the role of authority, the level of abstract thinking, and the intellectual freedom of the students is different in the four schools. The varying styles of hidden curriculum work to reproduce class by preparing children to occupy the same social and economic position as their parents. For example, in the working-class school, the students are taught to follow directions, obey authority, and get the right answers. In contrast, in the executive-elite school students are taught to make their own rules and find their own ways to solve problems. Each style builds skills and relationships in ways that perpetuate class by teaching students the skills and knowledge that will be needed for different class-based types of work and life.

River City

On any given weekend you are bound to find River City teenagers "hanging out" in old cars parked by the River. Driving around and visiting with friends is a common pastime for many of these teens. Some spend their weekends playing popular sports like hockey, football, and basketball. Many work at the local grocery store or shopping mall serving coffee or seating tables and taking a few hours away to spend time with their boyfriends or girlfriends. During the week, these young people attend their local high school, a place I call River City High School.* River City High School is located in a sprawling building made up of several different wings that have been tacked onto the original three-story structure. The school is located between a local elementary school and a shopping plaza. There are fast food chains and retail establishments dotting one of the roads leading up to the school, on other sides the school is bordered by residential areas.

Upon entering the high school, visitors are greeted by a security guard who directs them to the main office. Once inside, it is apparent that the school is alive with activity. Students pack the halls during the five minutes between bells, and often during classes, students will be in the halls outside of their classrooms working on projects. The building is crowded and many teachers share their classrooms with other teachers—some move to other rooms for their study halls or planning periods. The cafeteria is also small and there are lunch tables set up in the hall outside in order to accommodate all of the students.

---

* River City and River City High School are pseudonyms. All identifying names of people and places have been replaced with pseudonyms.

Despite the crowded nature of certain areas of the school, the building itself is sprawled out and includes a swimming pool, two gymnasiums (one old and one newer), and a new library with a computer lab. Behind the school, a green athletic field and track provide room for the school's athletes and physical education classes.

I have chosen River City High School for this study because its economic and cultural demographics make it a good fit for addressing my research questions, which revolve around what it means to be white and working class in a deindustrialized area and how young adults negotiate their own lives within the culture of the school and their economic setting.

River City is located just outside of a large Northeastern city I call Northtown. Though River City is not technically a suburb but a city, its economy is tied to Northtown's. Northtown is a city of almost 300,000 people whose economy has suffered in the past two decades due to the deindustrialization that has also impacted River City. Beginning in the 1970s and continuing today, many of Northtown's major manufacturing operations, including steel production, automobile manufacturing, and aircraft manufacturing, began laying off workers, and many of these industries eventually closed or moved leaving thousands jobless. The city continues to feel the impact of these economic blows today. As of 2000, Northtown's median household income was $24,536 compared to the national median of $41,994, and the number of families living below the poverty level was 23 percent compared to 9 percent nationally.[24] The region's largest employers are the state, county, and city governments, a healthcare company, an international bank, a motor vehicle parts manufacturer and the local state university.[25]

River City High School is located in a predominantly white, working-class city of 33,000 residents. The racial homogeneity of this city, where, according to the 2000 census, 97.9 percent of the residents were white, contrasts with nearby Northtown whose largest racial groups were whites, making up 54.4 percent of the population and blacks at 37.2 percent. River City has only one public high school which serves 1,680 students. Like its regional neighbors, the economy of River City has suffered in the past few decades. Because my study focuses largely on what it means to be working class, it is necessary to address the environment that the students and their families are a part of, both inside and outside of the school. While this study takes place within the school environment, the overall culture of the city and community is also an important factor in the lives of the students who are discussed.

Settled in the early 1800s, River City grew up around the logging industry, and after the lumber fields were depleted, it became a location for industrial growth. Industries like steel, paper, chemicals, and amusement park entertainment manufacturing moved in and thrived with the help of the railroads, which were being established across the country. Immigrants from Italy, Poland, Germany, Hungary and other counties moved into the area to fill the available jobs. However, as mentioned, the factory closings in the late twentieth century took their toll on this region that continues to suffer economically in the aftermath of this deindustrialization. Today, the largest employers in the city are the local hospital and the school district. However, the majority of students I interviewed had parents who worked outside of River City in the neighboring towns and cities. Parents who worked within River City were commonly employed in such fields as day care, retail, apartment management, and secretarial work.

River City's web site announces that today the city is focused on waterfront development, entertainment, and tourism. This focus on entertainment and tourism is not apparent when driving through, or even after spending time there. While there is one small section near the waterfront that houses quaint shops and small businesses, there are no substantial attractions that draw visitors from outside of the community, few hotels or motels, and little advertisement of the city itself or its businesses. In fact, River City is home to a number of abandoned industrial sites which are not only scars on the landscape but some also pose a threat to local health and the environment.[26]

In River City, the established working-class population shares the high school with a small number of middle-class families (conversation with Mr. Ferell, 2002). These middle-class families, referred to by Mr. Ferell, the guidance counselor, as "white collar" families, live in newer homes and developments mainly north of the high school. At the middle school level, students attend one of two middle schools. Smith Middle School is an older building and serves a population made up of mostly working-class families. It is located in a residential part of town near some of the city's older homes. Witter middle school is a more modern building with a large, green sports field and is located in a newer neighborhood of ranch-style houses. Both middle schools feed into the one public high school where I conducted my research, River City High School.

The 2000 Census reports that the median household income in this city is currently $35,154, up from $29,576 in 1990. The national median for 2000 was $41,994 and 30,056 in 1990. In 2000, most of these households fell into the $15,000 through $74,000 income brackets broken down as follows: 14.5 percent of families had an annual income between $15,000 and $24,999; 13.4 percent fell between $25,000 and $34,999; 18.7 percent fell between $35,000 and $49,000; 20.3 percent were between $50,000 and $74,999. Median earnings for male full-time, year-round workers were recorded as $36,551, while the same statistic for female workers was only $25,129.

The poverty threshold established by the census bureau for 2000 was $11,869 for a family of two adults and one child. According to Sklar, Mykyta & Wefald[27], a minimum needs budget for the same size family is $31,255 annually. A minimum needs budget reflects the fact that many Americans who are above government-established poverty lines still cannot provide for all of their families' basic needs. "The minimum needs budget includes the average cost of minimally adequate housing (including utilities), health care, food, child care, transportation, clothing and personal expenses, household expenses, telephone, and taxes—factoring in tax credits such as the Earned Income Credit and Child Tax Credit."[28]

The largest occupational groups in this area are management, professional, and related occupations, 29.8 percent; sales and office occupations 28.6 percent; production, transportation, and material moving occupations at 19.8 percent; followed by service occupations at 14.2 percent.[29] All groups—except for the first, management, professional, and related occupations—fall under the definition of working-class occupations, those where the workers have little autonomy or authority at work.

Even some of the "related occupations" in the first category also fall under this definition depending on the nature of the job, for example, nurse or purchasing agent.

The students I interviewed have parents, step-parents or guardians in the following list of occupations. The list does not represent individuals but the variety of occupational categories I found among all of the parents and guardians.

Mother, step-mother, female guardian:
Church worker (office and minor janitorial responsibilities)
Day care
Distribution
Factory work
Food service
Grocery store (deli, non-supervisory)
Health care (aide, technician, etc)
Management
Nursing
Optician
Retail
Secretarial
Stay-at-home mother
Teaching (requiring college degree and certification)
Waiting tables

Father, step-father, male guardian:
Apartment management (renting and maintaining one complex)
Business owner (construction)
Computer technician
Construction
Disabled (two fathers, formerly manual laborers)
Distribution
Factory work
Law enforcement
Maintenance
Mechanic
Military
Nursing
Secretarial
Plumber
Post office
Retired
Sales

This list, provided by the students I interviewed, gives an overall idea of the jobs held by this group of River City parents. The majority of the jobs listed here fall into the working-class category (twenty out of the thirty two categories). Other jobs such as military, stay-at-home mother, and law enforcement could fall into either working-class or middle-class categories depending on the exact duties, training, and authority each worker has on the job. Significantly, even with a few middle-class occupations listed, there are very few jobs that are solidly professional occupations where the worker has authority over his or her work. Where these do appear, they are found more often in the women's list (management and optician) than the men's. By coding these occupations as "working-class" and "middle-class," I do not want to imply that parent's occupations is the only standard being used to define class. As noted earlier, class is lived and practiced and includes social and cultural understandings and identities that go beyond one's relationship to the economy, or one's job and income. When these multiple considerations are taken into account, it allows us to understand class in terms of relationships. For example, the business owner, Mr. O'Brian, has a great deal of authority at his job as the owner of his own construction business, yet his relationships with those around him and other groups of people are reminiscent of traditional working-class hegemonic masculinities described in Willis's work.[30] For example, Mr. O'Brian exhibits an anti-authority stance, which led him to start his own business rather than work for someone else. He also is involved in racial boundary patrolling, setting his family in opposition to other racial groups which his daughter, Megan, explains later in Chapter Two as she discusses her secret relationship with her Puerto Rican boyfriend. In addition, while Mr. O'Brian's business is well established his family continually struggles with money and his daughter describes her family as "poor."

The River City community is one that has grown up around its industry as a racially and religiously homogeneous community. Racially and ethnically, the city is homogeneous; 97.9 percent of the city residents are white.[31] The student body mirrors this statistic with 98.5 percent of the high school students identifying themselves as white.[32]

Within the last twenty years, however, the community has begun to change. The loss of local manufacturing has caused a shift for River City's families. These working adults, many of whom are now parents of this generation of River City High School students, find themselves moving into jobs in a variety of fields. For some, especially those who pursue higher education, they move to management—and bureaucratic—type occupations. Others find their niche in service, sales, and retail while a few remain in the scarce manufacturing jobs which still exist in the surrounding areas.

Gaining Access to the School

The process of gaining access to the school was somewhat formal. Though contacts had given me names of teachers who might be willing to provide access to their classes, I was warned that before approaching them about this, I would need formal approval from the Board of Education because some teachers might be hesitant to allow a researcher into their classrooms without administrative permission. Before speaking to any of the teachers, I went through district and administrative channels to gain approval to work in the school. Once I gained this approval, most teachers and counselors were willing to talk to me and help me with my study. I owe special thanks to two teachers who helped me a great deal by welcoming me into their classrooms, on their fieldtrips, encouraging their students to work with me, allowing me to use their classroom for interviews, and including me in their social activities.

Data Collection

In order to successfully capture the intricacies and multiplicities of students' identity construction in this school setting, I use ethnography, non-participant and participant observation, interviews, and document analysis. I observed students in homerooms, various classes, study halls, in the halls before, during, and after school, and accompanied them on a fieldtrip. Observation also enables ethnographers to better understand what questions to ask and what issues are of importance in the everyday lives of the students, information that might not come out in a structured interview for which questions were written without prior observation of the site.

The research of Eckert, Proweller, Weiler, and Weis, for example, incorporates school-based ethnographic methodology.[33] The importance of going inside of the school to observe firsthand the actual everyday interactions of teachers, students, and administrators is central to these authors' discussions. The information obtained through observation not only allows the researcher to focus interview questions around pertinent topics, but it is unique and different from information gained through interviews alone and offers the opportunity to witness the ways students negotiate their school settings.

I also interacted with faculty and administrators in the faculty lounge, their classrooms, offices, and in some cases at their homes or local restaurants. My fieldwork was conducted over the course of nine months. Participant observation, non-participant observation, and interviews were my main focus and the primary sources of data gathering. I began by observing students during classes and school activities and compiled fieldnotes throughout my time in the school.

Observation and Participants

I began by observing three classes a day for three days a week. As the months progressed and I met more and more people at the school, I came in more than three days a week, observed different classes and talked with teachers in the teacher's lounge. I began by observing 11th-grade Regents social studies classes. Two were inclusion classes, which mix students labeled as "special education" students, non-labeled students and "college prep" track students into one learning environment. The inclusion classes were team-taught by a certified social studies teacher and a certified special education teacher. Non-inclusion classes were taught by one certified social studies teacher. The differently tracked students were not immediately identifiable in the inclusion classes, although they were often separated from other students during testing. On test days, special education students were taken to a separate room where many of them had one-on-one help with their tests from their teachers or aides. Some of the students, for example, had tests read aloud to them.

My objective upon entering the school was to meet as many different students as possible with the goal of being exposed to different groups of students in the school. By focusing my observations around three, and later four, different required classes, I was able to meet students who were in a variety of tracks in the school. From these original classes I then branched out by following students to other classes and school-based activities.

While I did not have access to any official student records, both students and teachers shared information as to whether students were in college-bound or vocational tracks, as well as information on what other academic and extra-curricular activities they took part in and their opinions of the students. I was also able to meet students from a variety of school cliques. After meeting students initially through selected classes I also talked with many teachers and some administrators in both informal and formal interviews (these were not tape-recorded, though details of these interactions were added to my fieldnotes).

The reason I focused on 11th grade classes is because the 11th grade year is a significant time when students are often making decisions about what they will do after high school. During this year students choose whether or not to take the SATs and/or ACTs and college-bound students often begin thinking about specific schools they would like to attend. I hoped to interview students who had done some thinking and talking about their post-high school futures outside of my interview. Though most high school students are asked to think about these issues very early on, it is usually not until 11th grade that guidance counselors begin to talk to students about the college selection and application process.

Interviews

The months that I spent observing and interacting with the students served the dual purposes of providing me with ethnographic information and allowing me to get to know students and become comfortable and accepted within the school setting before approaching individual students for one-on-one interviews. Most of my interviews were done with students I met in the four different social studies classes that I observed throughout the year. Individual interviews were conducted with twenty-seven students; fourteen boys and thirteen girls. The students selected were from a variety of different groups around the school with the goal of selecting small groups of students from different tracks, with different interests, and from different peer groups. I also wanted to interview roughly the same number of boys and girls in order to get a better idea about how the school culture was negotiated by each of these groups.

I opened the interview process to the students and asked for volunteers by first explaining my project to the classes, similar to what I had done when I introduced myself upon entering the classes. I talked about where I was from, that I was doing research about the lives of eleventh graders, and gave them a few examples of the types of questions I would ask in my interviews. Two of the teachers I worked with were generous enough to allow me to do this during class time. At this time, I also passed out consent forms and a short written questionnaire which asked simplified versions of my interview questions, both of which I asked students to return to me as soon as possible. Again, the teachers were helpful by asking students to drop the papers in a basket in the classroom, which allowed students to leave these for me even if I was not in their class that day.

The short written questionnaire was particularly helpful to me when selecting students for interviews. It also served the purpose of reinforcing for me that the population I was dealing with did indeed fit the economic and racial profile for which I had selected the school. All students but one who completed my questionnaire were white—the other was Puerto Rican. While almost all of the students completed the written questionnaire, only a handful volunteered for the interviews.

I began by interviewing the volunteers and then approached students one-on-one to participate. Using snowball sampling, I asked interviewees for names of other students who might be interested and then approached those students about doing interviews with me. I also reviewed the questionnaires and chose potential interviewees from these. From the questionnaires, I choose students from a variety of different academic and social groups (i.e. students from different tracks and different cliques) within the school. As noted earlier, one of my objectives is to address multiple student perspectives. After observing in River City High School for six months before conducting my interviews with students, it was easy for me to identify which social and academic groups students belonged to. For example, students' clothing often signified which cliques they belonged to. Athletes, both male and female, frequently wore their uniforms or parts of their uniforms to school, usually on game days. Cheerleaders often wore accessories such as hair ribbons in the school colors. Certain other groups of students wore symbolic clothing that was labeled by the students as "punk," "prep," or "hippie" attire. "Punk" attire might include black clothing, t-shirts depicting certain bands and often personalized by being cut or written on and accessories such as "dog collar" style necklaces. "Prep" attire often included jeans and sweatshirts or t-shirts from certain popular stores such as Abercrombie and Fitch, Hollister, and Aeropostale. Often this clothing prominently displayed the logos of these companies. "Hippie" attire included worn jeans and t-shirts, particularly t-shirts depicting rock bands from the 1970s such as Led Zepplin, and distinctive long haircuts, particularly for boys who wore their hair below the collar line, often in a messy style. In addition, teachers often offered their opinions about students and told me things like, "You should interview Casey, I think you would find it interesting."

I approached the individual students by again explaining my project, giving them some examples of questions I would be asking and assuring them that their identities would be protected and things they told me would not be shared with their teachers. I told them that I was using this information to write my dissertation and gave the consent form to those who did not already have it from class. Almost all of the students I approached one-on-one agreed to do interviews with me. I arranged the interviews around the students' schedules by conducting the interviews during their study halls, lunch periods, and before and after school.

All interviews were conducted on school grounds, either before, during, or after school. The locations of the interviews varied due to which spaces were available and private at the time. Most of the interviews were conducted in a special resource room. This room was a very large, windowless space broken up into about twelve cubicles by office-style dividers with one central space containing a few round tables. Other interviews were done in the library or empty classrooms; one was done in the empty cafeteria.

The interviews consisted largely of open-ended questions and while my questions remained generally the same I experimented, especially in the first interviews, with different wording and different question order. For example, with students who I knew were interested in a certain sport or activity, I began with those questions and moved into the interview from there. This was mainly an attempt to put students at ease but also to start the flow of conversation by allowing students to begin the conversation talking about something they were not only interested in, but were often knowledgeable about. If a certain point of topic came up that I wanted to learn more about, I left the interview questions momentarily to follow up on that topic.

The interviews varied from forty-five minutes to an hour and a half. The questions centered on the role the school plays in the students' perceptions of self, their role in society, and their future aspirations. All interviews with students were tape-recorded and later transcribed.

Data Analysis

The transcribed data and fieldnotes were coded and analyzed. The seventy codes used were derived both from my leading question and subquestions, as well as from patterns and themes identified from the fieldnotes and interviews. The guiding research questions include: How do white working-class youth construct class and gendered and racial identities? What role does the school play in the construction, understanding, and articulation of these identities? How do students articulate their school-based peer culture and their relationships with other agencies outside of school? How do the students position themselves and view themselves within the larger social and economic setting? What role do these perceptions play in their understanding of their own futures, specifically focusing on educational, occupational, and family goals?

An example of a code derived from general questions is "future career" which was used to code sections in which students talked about what job or career they wanted to pursue or envisioned themselves pursuing in the future. This directly connects with the more general question of how students see themselves and position themselves within the larger social world. An example of a code which was derived from specific interview data is "abuse." Abuse was something I did not specifically address in my leading research questions or even specifically in my open-ended interview questions, which focus more generally on the students' family situation.

However, after hearing stories of abuse from some students, I determined it was a significant factor in their lives which impacted how they thought about family, gendered relationships, and education and generated the code "abuse" to address this. When coding both fieldnotes and interviews careful attention was paid to both the similarities and differences between articulations and actions.[34]

In addition to my fieldnotes and interviews, I also collected documents while I was at River City High School. I collected many of the papers and worksheets that were handed out in classes where I was observing. In addition, I collected materials on the college application process that were given to junior year students by their guidance counselors.

Organization of Chapters

Finally, I have written my findings up in the form of chapters. The discussions which follow grow out of the analysis of identity construction and the formation of group identities in River City high school. Identity is a complicated and multi-faceted topic and can include many aspects of discussion. I have chosen to focus on class, gender, race, and peer groups as significant categories because during my fieldwork and interviews, these categories emerged as significant in the lives of the students and the culture of the school. Other categories are certainly significant, as well, and many of these are touched on within the following chapters. However, the highlighted topics were chosen because of the way they help to explain some of the unique aspects of the school culture and clarify the ways that the official school curriculum is entwined with the hidden curriculum, student culture, and community as a whole.

This chapter included an explanation of the main questions, a brief review of pertinent literature, and a description of methods. The next chapter, Chapter Two, reports on the girls of River City High School and discusses and interprets their family situations and how these impact the way the girls think about their own futures in terms of educational pursuits, economic considerations, and family situations. Incorporating their own voices, I present what the girls have to say about their lives, the lives of their families and what they think about their futures. Situated in a changing economic and educational landscape, the girls conceptualize their futures in different ways than prior generations have, yet in doing this, they express a keen regard for the personal histories of their families and their mother's lives, in particular. The girls focus on the resilience of their mothers, how hard they work and how they have struggled with their jobs, educations, and families.

After discussing the girls, I move my attention to the boys in Chapter Three. The boys' dialogues and concerns are markedly distinct from those of the girls. While the girls focused on the strength of their mothers, few of the boys expressed the same personalized, intense connection with their parents' lives and struggles. The boys viewed their futures not so much as connected to the lessons of their families or the need to be better prepared for life's challenges than their parents, but saw their choices as the result of individual accomplishment. The boys, many of whom were the first generation in their families who planned to attend college, spoke of careers which were related to their own ambitions. In general, the boys expected to work, have families, and own a house in contrast to the girls who focus on their careers first, then marriage and family.

In Chapter Four, I discuss the peer groups in River City High School. In the absence of racial or marked economic differences within the high school population, the students cited peer groups as the way that students were divided within the school. Peer groups, marked by semiotic devices such as clothing, language use, and visibility in the school, were the main way students talked about and identified themselves and each other within the culture of the school. Peer groups mark students' relationships with the authority structure of the school and connect to a system of school-sanctioned rewards for students who conform and participate.

The discussion in Chapter Five turns to race and the ways that it is both invisible and normalized within this racially homogenous environment. This chapter builds off of the peer group discussion presented in Chapter Four and extends the discussion of group identities. Masked by a dialogue of "normality" and "sameness," the students express their ideas about where they are situated, both racially and economically. This dialogue of normality allows a space for these students to construct their identities as neither privileged nor underprivileged, a view that may have unpredictable implications, particularly for those who venture outside of their somewhat insulated community.

Finally, I conclude with a comprehensive discussion that weaves these spheres together as critical components in identity formation. I consider the ways in which all of these components play a part in the identities of these students as they reflect on their future aspirations in conversation with me and as they interact with teachers, administrators, and other students within the structured setting of the school. Lastly, I consider the implications of the findings.

Notes

1. Willis, Paul. *Learning to Labor: How Working Class Kids Get Working Class Jobs.* New York: Columbia University Press, 1977.

2. Bluestone, B., and B. Harrison. *The Deindustrialization of America: Plant Closings, Community Abandonment, and the Dismantling of Basic Industry.* New York: Basic Books, 1982; Bluestone, B. and B. Harrison. *Growing Prosperity: the Battle for Growth with Equity in the Twenty-First Century.* Boston: Houghton Mifflin Company, 2000; Ehrenreich, B. *Nickel and Dimed: On (Not) Getting by in America.* New York: Metropolitan Books, 2001; Rubin, L. *Families on the Fault Line: America's Working Class Speaks About the Family, the Economy, Race and Ethnicity.* New York: Harper Collins, 1994; Sklar, H. *Chaos of Community: Seeking Solutions, Not Scapegoats for Bad Economics.* Boston: South End Press, 1995.

3. Ehrenreich, B. *Nickel and Dimed: On (Not) Getting by in America.* New York: Metropolitan Books, 2001.

4. Keister, L. *Wealth in America: Trends in Wealth Inequality.* Cambridge: Cambridge University Press, 2000; Rubin, L. *Worlds of Pain: Life in the Working-Class Family.* New

York: Basic Books, 1976; Rubin, L. *Families on the Fault Line: America's Working Class Speaks About the Family, the Economy, Race and Ethnicity.* New York: Harper Collins, 1994; Sklar, H. *Chaos of Community: Seeking Solutions, Not Scapegoats for Bad Economics.* Boston: South End Press, 1995; Reich, R. *I'll Be Short: Essentials for a Decent Working Society.* Boston: Beacon Press, 2002.

   5. Mantsios, G. "Class in America - 2003." In *Race, Class and Gender in the United States: An Integrated Study,* edited by P. Rothenberg. New York: St. Martin's Press, 2004. 196.

   6. Zweig, M. *The Working Class Majority: America's Best Kept Secret.* Ithaca: Cornell University Press, 2000. 72.

   7. Weis, L. *Class Reunion: The Remaking of the American White Working Class.* New York: Routledge, 2004.

   8. McLaren, P., and V. Scatamburlo-D'Annibale. "Paul Willis, Class Consciousness, and Critical Pedagogy: Toward a Socialist Future." In *Learning to Labor in New Times,* edited by N. Dolby and G. Dimitriadis. New York: RoutledgeFalmer, 2004.

   9. Zweig, M. *The Working Class Majority: America's Best Kept Secret.* Ithaca: Cornell University Press, 2000. 1.

   10. Reich, R. *The Work of Nations: Preparing Ourselves for 21st Century Capitalism.* Albany: SUNY Press, 1997.

   11. Zweig, M., ed. *What's Class Got to Do with It? American Soceity in the Twenty-First Century.* Ithaca and London: ILR Press and imprint of Cornell University Press, 2004.

   12. Bourdieu in MacLeod, J. *Ain't No Makin' It: Aspirations and Attainment in a Low-Income Neighborhood.* Boulder: Westview Press Inc., 1995.

   13. Reich, R. *The Work of Nations: Preparing Ourselves for 21st Century Capitalism.* Albany: SUNY Press, 1997.

   14. Anyon, J. "Social Class and School Knowledge." *Curriculum Inquiry* 11, no. 1 (1981): 3-42.

   15. Finn, P. J. *Literacy with an Attitude: Educating Working-Class Children in Thier Own Self Interest.* Albany: SUNY Press, 1999.

   16. Weis, L. *Class Reunion: The Remaking of the American White Working Class.* New York: Routledge, 2004.

   17. Gaskell, J. *Gender Matters: From School to Work.* Philadelphia: Open University Press, 1992; McRobbie, A. "Working Class Girls and the Culture of Femininity." In *Women Take Issue: Aspects of Women's Subordination,* edited by CCCS. London: Hutchinson, 1978; Willis, P. *Learning to Labor: How Working Class Kids Get Working Class Jobs.* New York: Columbia University Press, 1977; Weis, L. *Working Class without Work: High School Students in a Deindustrializing Economy.* New York: Routledge, 1990.

   18. Weis, L. *Class Reunion: The Remaking of the American White Working Class.* New York: Routledge, 2004.

   19. Willis, P. *Learning to Labor: How Working Class Kids Get Working Class Jobs.* New York: Columbia University Press, 1977.

   20. Willis, P. *Learning to Labor: How Working Class Kids Get Working Class Jobs.* New York: Columbia University Press, 1977; McRobbie, A. "Working Class Girls and the Culture of Femininity." In *Women Take Issue: Aspects of Women's Subordination,* edited by CCCS. London: Hutchinson, 1978; Eckert, P. *Jocks and Burnouts: Social Categories and Identity in High School.* New York: Teachers College Press, 1989; Holland, D., and M. Eisenhart. *Educated in Romance: Women, Achievement, and College Culture.* Chicago: University of Chicago Press, 1990; Weis, L. *Working Class without Work: High School Students in a Deindustrializing Economy.* New York: Routledge, 1990; Gaskell, J. *Gender Matters: From School to Work.* Philadelphia: Open University Press, 1992; Proweller, A. *Constructing Identities:*

Meaning Making in an Upper Middle Class Youth Culture. New York: State University of New York Press, 1998; Perry, P. *Shades of White: White Kids and Racial Identities in High School*. Durham: Duke University Press, 2002.

21. Weis, L. *Class Reunion: The Remaking of the American White Working Class*. New York: Routledge, 2004.

22. Bowles, S., and H. Gintis. *Schooling in Capitalist America: Educational Reform and the Contradictions of Economic Life*. New York: Basic Books, 1976.

23. Anyon, J. "Social Class and School Knowledge." *Curriculum Inquiry* 11, no. 1 (1981): 3-42.

24. "United States Census." 2000.

25. Region's Largest Employers. 2004. In Local Development Association. (accessed 2004).

26. "Hazardous Waste Sites in Our County." *River City South News* 2000

27. Sklar, H., L. Mykyta, and S. Wefald. *Raise the Floor: Wages and Policies That Work for All of Us*. New York: Ms. Foundation for Women, 2001.

28. Sklar, H., L. Mykyta, and S. Wefald. *Raise the Floor: Wages and Policies That Work for All of Us*. New York: Ms. Foundation for Women, 2001.

29. "United States Census." 2000.

30. Willis, Paul. *Learning to Labor: How Working Class Kids Get Working Class Jobs*. New York: Columbia University Press, 1977.

31. "United States Census." 2000.

32. "New York State Report Card 2001-2002." 2002.

33. Eckert, P. *Jocks and Burnouts: Social Categories and Identity in High School*. New York: Teachers College Press, 1989; Proweller, A. *Constructing Identities: Meaning Making in an Upper Middle Class Youth Culture*. New York: State University of New York Press, 1998; Weiler, J.D. *Codes and Contradictions: Race, Gender Identity, and Schooling*. Albany: SUNY Press, 2000; Weis, L. *Working Class without Work: High School Students in a Deindustrializing Economy*. New York: Routledge, 1990.

34. Bogdan, R., and S. K. Bicklin. *Qualitative Research for Education: An Introduction to Theory and Methods*. Boston: Allyn and Bacon Inc., 1982.

Chapter Two

Girls at River City High School

My mom taught me everything . . . She always teaches me everything that she never had. She tells me, she's like 'I always want you to be better than I ever was,' stuff like that.

Gwen—age seventeen

Within the largely economically and racially homogeneous community of River City, students are still divided along multiple lines and one of the most salient of these is gender. Gender lines are clearly visible and are reinforced by the school and students.

Gender distinctions become particularly pronounced in the ways girls and boys talk about their families and domestic futures. Notably, the ways girls envision their futures with respect to education, family and career as they reflect on life experiences and future plans are different from those of the boys. This chapter focuses on what the girls from River City expect from their futures and how the school and family cultures they are a part of, as well as their gendered identities, contribute to these perceptions.

Specifically, this chapter considers the ways in which white working-class girls from River City interpret and articulate the struggles of their mothers. How do these struggles with relationships, education, and jobs, play out in the girls' lives? How do the girls envision their own futures in light of the struggles they have witnessed and, often, of which they have been a part?

Work by McRobbie and Holland and Eisenhart has analyzed how young girls construct their futures around a romantic ideal that often leads them to focus on the domestic sphere.[1] Weis's *Working Class Without Work* found that white working-class girls in the 1980s exhibited moments of critique of just such a romantic ideal. The girls in Weis's study were critical of marriage in particular and articulated the necessity for a woman to be able to support herself in light of an economy that could no longer guarantee their male cohorts employment, much less employment which could provide enough income to support a family and allow a wife to stay home and raise the children. The girls at River City High articulate a similar critique, and by reflecting on their own mothers' struggles with family, education and career, the girls highlight the necessity for strength, education, and especially self-reliance.

Numerous other studies have focused on gender and schooling and many more have incorporated discussions of gender roles in school. For example, Gaskell studies stratification in schools and the role of tracking.[2] She incorporates ideas about

21

hidden curriculum within the school and the role of peer culture in creating and per-petuating gender role expectations. Her attention is focused on gender and the inter-section of class and gender. Her study of gender and course choice illustrates specifi-cally how traditional gender roles are reinforced by schools and student culture through course choice. Gaskell shows how young women and young men are steered, and steer themselves, toward different courses. The young men in Gaskell's study are encouraged to pursue courses such as wood shop while young women enroll in typing or home economics. [3] A similar pattern of young women preferring so-called "soft" subjects like English and social studies while young men prefer the "hard" subjects such as science and math has also received attention. [4]

In addition to analyzing the role of the school in gender reproduction, Gaskell conducted interviews with Canadian working-class high school students in the mid-1980s. She found that although many of the young women planned on working out-side of the home, they saw this work as secondary both to their domestic duties and to their future husband's paid work. Alternately, the young men Gaskell interviewed cling uncritically to traditional working-class notions of family and work that were demonstrated by their parents. Gaskell identifies three main factors that contribute to the perpetuation of traditional notions of gender roles among these students: the young men's attitudes and self-interest, the structure of the labor market in which women's jobs pay less than men's, and inadequate options for childcare. In envision-ing their futures, the students employ these three themes and come to conclusions in line with a conservative working-class ideology.

Work, like Gaskell's, focusing on the reproduction of gender within the school setting, highlights the variability of gender roles. McRobbie, Weiler, and Proweller each describe the reproduction of gender in different school settings. [5] McRobbie focuses on the intersection of class, and gender in her analysis of white working-class girls. Weiler works at the intersection of race, class, and gender while paying close attention to race and ethnicity in the alternative school setting she investigates. Proweller's focus is a space of class privilege, and she highlights the ways race and gender impact identity within this setting.

McRobbie's work expands on Paul Willis's by addressing the young women who were largely overlooked by Willis. [6] Her focus is on the contradictions within the young women's culture and the ways in which they act out their sexuality within school as an assertion of their resistance to authority. Similar to the boys', the girls' culture, which stresses sexuality and romance, works to reproduce traditional gender roles.

Weiler analyzes student culture as it is articulated and acted out within the school setting, yet her work also focuses on class and race/ethnicity as factors that contribute to girls' identity formation during adolescence. [7] She discusses working-class young women of different racial and ethnic backgrounds who attend an alterna-tive high school. Weiler's focus is on the complicated ways in which peer culture, class background, racial/ethnic background, and alternative-school culture interact and how the students coming from this setting express their hopes and goals for the future.

Within the group of white working-class young women, Weiler identifies three basic orientations toward the future: those who focus on family life as inevitable and only vaguely consider a career, those who consider family life as primary and have a secondary interest in a career, and those who are committed to careers. She highlights the complexity of responses derived from one group of working-class young women. This work illustrates not only the multiple identities and views within one group labeled as working class, but the ways in which high school education, the perceived availability of college education, and the perception of career options are negotiated with traditional domestic ideologies.

Like Weiler's study, mine too discusses the school as a site for both formal instruction and social interaction and the formation of student culture that influences racial, class, and gender identity. I also discuss the ways in which girls envision their future negotiations between family and career. Yet unlike Weiler's study, my own work addresses the experiences of boys as well as girls.

Proweller's work is a comprehensive study of identity development in an elite, private, all-girls school.[8] She incorporates ethnographic methods in her study of the everyday lives of these girls and the ways they make meaning out of their experiences and understand themselves in terms of gender, race, education and social class. Proweller focuses on identity formation within a structured school setting. Of particular interest are the ways the girls make use of school-sanctioned groups and rituals to construct their identities. Proweller's small, elite setting is very different from where my work is conducted and provides important contrasts, as well as interesting similarities regarding ways students construct meaningful group identities within a largely adult-dictated environment.

Like both Weiler and Proweller, this study works to understand identity development as a multifaceted and complicated practice that centers around the struggle to understand oneself in relation to the world and specifically in connection with the agencies, institutions, and relationships that make up everyday life. Central to the discussion are the factors of class, gender, and race. Although there are certainly other factors of importance, my analysis focuses on these three. Class, gender, and race are significant and well-studied aspects of identity that I use as a foundation for my discussion of white working-class student identity. Using this foundation, I also discuss other aspects of identity that emerged as salient during analysis. Class, gender, and race are also particularly significant because people often identify themselves, coalesce, and separate themselves using these ideas. In addition, societies, agencies, and schools are largely stratified along the lines of class, gender, and race.

Holland and Eisenhart's *Educated in Romance* explores similar themes to those discussed in McRobbie's and Gaskell's work, but Holland and Eisenhart focus on college-level women. In a comparison of southern colleges, Holland and Eisenhart find a pervasive culture of romance in which young women often find their academic plans derailed by romantic pursuits. The authors highlight some strategies that women use to negotiate the social atmospheres of the campuses that generally revolve around male/female relationships. They point out how the ideology of romance and attractiveness proves a distracting force for many women. Men, on the other hand, hold a privileged position in gender relations; their social status and perceptions of self are not as dependent on being attractive or romantically involved as the women's.

Holland and Eisenhart's work focuses primarily on campus peer culture and the ways in which it works against women's educational goals. Even the women who develop strategies that help them separate themselves from social pressures to be romantically involved still are not exempt from the culture of attractiveness and femininity. Though some of the women in this study were able to finish their education and minimize the pressures of the culture of romance, others found their education eclipsed by the culture.[9]

Gendered identities are negotiated with different outcomes for groups across time, class, race, and education. Girls in particular face frequently contradictory expectations regarding family and career. Yet while much attention has been given to women and girls, it is also necessary to acknowledge the ways that both men's and women's lives impact one another. As girls rethink the role of a woman, wife, and mother, men too are rethinking their multiple roles both in relation and response to social and economic pressures.

This chapter presents what the River City High girls have to say about their futures in light of the struggles of their mothers which they have not only seen, but have lived through and in many cases participated in as well. These articulations point at a new class-based view of gender roles which necessitates reworking traditional roles if one wants to overcome, or even avoid, some of the struggles the previous generation faced. This chapter also explores the ways the girls address education and its role in their future plans.

The Resilient Mother: Coping in a World Without Guarantees

In one-on-one interviews many of the girls at River City highlighted their relationships with their mothers and for the most part said positive things about these relationships. While some of the girls also discussed their fathers, they did not nearly as often refer to shared struggles and life stories when speaking about their fathers. Reflecting on their relationships with their mothers, the girls talked about struggles around the sites of education, job, and family relationships, which they witnessed and often shared with their mothers, and how these struggles impact their lives.

The girls have seen their mothers, and other women in their lives, struggle in different ways. These struggles revolve around the sites of education, jobs, and families. Many of the girls talk about the resiliency, strength, and determination of the women in their lives and the ways they are coping with challenges and reflect on these challenges, at least partly, as connected to their gendered roles. Particularly, the girls connect these stories of struggle with their thoughts about future responsibilities as women and mothers who will be in positions to provide for themselves and their children.

Despite the realization of the gendered aspect of many of the life struggles that their families face, few of the girls are able to reflect on these personal struggles as ones intimately attached to their class and the larger economy.

Maria's story is one example of balancing a critique that contrasts economic considerations with dreams and talents when choosing what to pursue in the future.

Maria

Maria is a petite cheerleader and dancer with short brown hair and seemingly endless energy. She is constantly experimenting with her hairstyle and clothing, which usually consists of jeans and t-shirts, often decorated with designer names or colorful and shiny appliqués. She is quiet in class but talkative around her friends. Maria usually gets good grades in her classes and is well liked by her teachers. Though she cheered this year, a falling out with the cheerleading coach led her to decide not to try out for the squad next year. While she fears that this might strain her friendships with her friends who are cheerleaders, she is adamant about her decision.

Maria, whose mother just divorced her step-father six months before this conversation, speaks about her mother, who is an elementary school teacher.

> *Maria: My mom tried to teach me that to get something you have to work hard. School has always been very important for me. That's always been the basis, like you need to do good in school to get somewhere. Good grades have always been important.*

Maria talks about the divorce . . .

> *Maria: My parents just got divorced about six months ago. That was a good thing actually. He [step-father] wasn't a healthy person; he was a toxic person in our house. He wasn't a pleasant person but they were married for eight years and then, which is, the last three years, my mom and dad didn't agree on anything. And I know it wasn't my fault but there was a lot of issues with me, like, growing up and getting older and being a teenager [. . .] It's pretty hard for my little sister because that's her dad, you know. It's my step-dad so it wasn't really, I didn't really have any connection, not connection, but any, even knowing how bad your dad is, that's still your dad. No matter what he did, that's still your dad. She's having a hard time with it.*

Maria talks about her mother as a very important and central part of her life. Their shared struggles, including the death of Maria's biological father followed by her mother's difficult second marriage and messy divorce, allow Maria to envision herself and her mother as sharing common struggles around their gendered roles. The lesson of self-reliance or, more accurately, not having to rely on a man for support, which has grown out of experiences like this one, lead teenage girls like Maria to gravitate toward a practical plan of self-reliance.

Here, she discusses her own and her mother's practical concerns when it comes to choosing a career. Maria is an accomplished dancer who also teaches classes at the dance studio she attends.

> *Carrie: Do you plan on dancing when you go to college?*
> *Maria: [. . .] I keep thinking 'do I want to or don't I?' If I could I would teach. I would teach. That's all I would do. I would love to teach, that would be my job, as a dance teacher. And open my own studio and be the owner. That would be my, that's what I want to do but I can't. I just, I don't think I could. I'm more like, like I plan. I want a stable job. That's what I want. My dance teacher, her husband makes all the money. There's no problem like, 'How did you do with health insurance [. . .]?' Dance instructors, it's not there. That's only my concern and my mom never really, she never said, 'No, you can't do that,' but she's like, 'Here's what happens.' And I always wanted a stable job and stable money coming in. I want something set. I don't, you know, they don't have contracts.*

Though Maria "would love to teach [dance]," she has instead decided to pursue a career in something related to psychology. Her mother, who is very involved in her college selection process which began this year, has warned her that being a dance teacher will likely not be economically practical for her, and Maria agrees. Maria looks at her own dance teacher, who owns her studio, but she remarks that, "her husband makes all the money." Maria is not counting on the fact that she will necessarily have a husband, or a husband who will make enough money to support her. Therefore, she has opted for what she and her mother see as a practical career option. It is quite clear that Maria will have to provide for herself during and after college. Maria's mothers' research around the college selection process is focused on not only choosing a school but finding a way to pay for it and scholarships have been one of their main foci.

In addition, given the many Americans now living without healthcare, Maria's concerns over having insurance are very realistic, particularly in light of some health issues she has encountered recently. In 2002, 43.6 million Americans had no health insurance for that year.[10]

Still, Maria continues to talk about possibly returning to dancing when she is older and able to provide for herself.

> *Maria: If I can, when I'm older, if I can I'll teach on the side. That's what I would love to do. That's something that maybe would come into play if I could but right now psychology is my main thing.*

Maria's decision to focus on a career that will be better paying, more stable, and offer more benefits than dancing is directly related to her class and life experience, as well as that of her mother. Despite the fact that Maria's mother is one of the few mothers from this group who graduated from college, for her, the purpose of higher education is in line with this group overall, stressing the importance of the credential and its role in getting a good-paying job.

Amanda

Amanda's mother and step-father are also in the process of divorcing. Amanda is an outwardly confident and enthusiastic girl with long dark, curly hair. She frequently volunteers to read aloud in class, something most students shy away from. She is actively involved in drama club, chorus, and animal club. Her closest friends are not students at River City High but people she has met through her involvement in theater. Amanda's dream is to work in musical theater on Broadway. Here, she talks about her relationship with her mother and sister.

> *Amanda: I don't know, I'm just kind of glad we're moving. It's just going to be me and my sister and my mom again. Just, like how it always was and how I want it, so.*
> *Carrie: It was that way before she got married?*
> *Amanda: Yeah, it was that way before, it was just us, it was great. I mean she was dating people in and out. I never really had a stable father but, like, you know, she was just, she's a great mom. It was just better when it was just us girls. Because girls understand each other better than any guy would. So, I'm kind of happy.*

Amanda has been through some difficult times with her mother and now will be moving to Florida for her senior year of high school, as a result of the divorce. Amanda, facing many changes in her life, views her mother and sister as her basic family unit. She talks about the importance of their bond as "girls" and notes that, "It was just better when it was just us girls." Her reaction to her mother's divorce is very similar to Maria's and both express the idea that somehow things are now returning to normal and will be better as a result of the divorce. Both girls also realize that there will be upcoming struggles and the females in their families will stick together through these tough times.

Amanda speaks about her mother's struggles with education and employment.

> *Amanda: She dropped out of high school at the age of sixteen. I know that's not really anything to look up to but, I'm happy with everything she's doing now. She's a good parent. She tries so hard to be a mom, keep a job, you know, this and that. She got her GED. Oh my God she was so happy when she got her GED. She's graduated from high school now, which is good.*
> *Carrie: Did she get her GED recently?*

> *Amanda: No, like two years ago. It was really exciting, I was all happy for her. She was like, 'I'm going to go back to college when I have time.' You know, raising two kids, and she had to raise a husband, which is even weirder, it was just kind of like, when do you have time to go back to college? You don't!*

Amanda has grown up seeing her mother raise two daughters and keep jobs, without even the benefit of a high school education. She revels in her mother's accomplishments, earning her GED and holding down a job, and she sympathizes with her mother's struggles such as postponing a college education and paying off debts.

Despite the fact that Amanda supports her mother's decision to divorce, she also realizes that the move to Florida will likely negatively impact her plans for the future. After talking about some of the things she will miss, like her jet ski and the house, she talks through some of her ideas about what she will do after high school.

> *Amanda: Basically after high school in Harborhill, because that's where I'll be graduating from, I plan on taking one year off. I know everybody says not to do that and originally I wasn't. I was going to go to a two-year school in New York because I knew Regents were going to kill me, and I have to get up my average because it's not that high, so I was going to go to River City Community College for about two years, get my training done, get my grades caught up and then attend a bigger college. Go on to a four-year school. But since my plans all got messed up with this moving thing I have to take a year off to audition because there are so many opportunities in Florida, you don't even know. I mean there are so many. I could do anything there.*
>
> *But my main plan is to take a year off, audition for everything, if I don't make it I'm going to college. I'm going straight from high school to college. I don't know how. Obviously with a job I'll be able to pay for college better because I know my mom's going to be tight on money. This whole family is going to be tight on money. So I just gotta take a year off and work on getting my own money to pay for college. I know I have to do that. That's just my main thing. I'm just going to take one thing at a time, one year at a time, so basically after next year, working, working, working and then going to college to further my education and stuff.*

Amanda comes to the conclusion that she will have to work her way through college, which likely will include taking a year off, because, "This whole family [her mother, her younger sister, and herself] is going to be tight on money." At the same time as Amanda realizes that she cannot count on her family to pay for her college education, she seems committed to sharing the future struggles she, her mother and sister will likely encounter as they move into a new phase of life without her step-father or much of the economic support he provided.

In Amanda's situation, which is similar to that of many of the River City teens, she expresses reluctance to rely on student loans to finance her college education, instead discussing working her way through school or postponing higher education for work opportunities. The overall reluctance to take student loans or to go into debt to pursue higher education is common among both the working-class girls and boys who shared their stories with me. A similar view of student debt was found in Bloom's work with impoverished students of color.[11] This reluctance is an interesting statement about these groups' unwillingness to take on personal debt in light of a perceived value of higher education. It can also be read as a statement about the actual availability of education, which diminishes considerably when a group of people feels priced-out of this opportunity.

Though both Maria's and Amanda's stories involve recent divorces, my intention is not to imply that all River City High School students come from homes that have experienced divorce. Nor is divorce the only circumstance under which girls are able to identify with their mother's lives and struggles. Divorce is one of the many life changes which can bring with it economic struggle, particularly for women with children.

Alicia

Alicia is a very quiet girl who usually wears jeans and t-shirts with the names of rock bands on them. Her short hair is bleached blonde and a lock near her face has alternated between orange and pink at different times during the year. Alicia struggles in school and has been diagnosed with a learning disability. She lives with both of her parents, who are married. Her older brother lives next door. Like Maria and Amanda, she identifies with her mother's struggles, which involve her job and continuing education.

Alicia is very close with her mother. When I ask her if she has a role model, she answers,

> *Alicia: My mom.*
> *Carrie: Your mom, why?*
> *Alicia: I just, I look up to her and stuff. She's just the best . . .*

At this point in the interview Alicia begins to cry as she reflects on her relationship with her mother and the closeness they share. Alicia's social life outside of school revolves around her interest in music and as an active fan of many bands. She sometimes contacts the bands' promoters through web sites and helps to pass out flyers and stickers before shows. Her hobby of attending shows and meeting band members is one sometimes associated with drinking and taking drugs. However, Alicia tells me she chooses not to drink alcohol or take drugs and explains her choice as a result of her parents' attitudes. She tells me that their support and acceptance of her have led her to make this choice.

> *Alicia: I do not drink. My mom and dad, if I ever do, they'd be okay with it. They won't ground me, they won't do anything. Which is, I don't really drink, I find it hard to.*

Like Alicia, Maria's attitude towards drugs and alcohol has developed with consideration for her close relationship with her mother. Maria also cites this as a reason she does not drink often and has felt guilty in the past when she has because she knows her mother trusts her to be responsible.

Both of Alicia's parents are now in college for the first time, as well as working full-time. Her father works with computers and her mother works as a secretary at the local headquarters of an international bank. Although both her parents find themselves in similar situations, Alicia talks a great deal more about her mother's plight than her father's. Similar to most of the girls who spoke with me, Alicia identifies with her mother on more than one level. Alicia explains how her mother is pursuing her degree in an attempt to keep her job as the company she works for continues to move jobs to India.

> *Carrie: Did they go to college [your parents]?*
> *Alicia: They're going to college now.*
> *Carrie: Your parents are going to college now? What made them decide to do that?*
> *Alicia: My mom's job is like moving people off to India, and my mom needs a higher degree or they'll move her out. So she is, and my dad, I don't know.*

Though Alicia talks about how smart her mother is and how she is good at her job, she sees her job being threatened. Her mother's struggle to keep her job has led her to enroll in college while still working full-time. Like other mothers of River City teens who work more than one job, Alicia's mother has to work hard to hold on to her secretarial job. This leaves Alicia with extra responsibilities at home such as looking after her little sister.

Alicia is one of the few girls who is beginning to form a social critique based on her mother's situation. She directly connects the threat to her mother's livelihood that has forced her back to school as a part of a larger economic global trend which includes the outsourcing of jobs. Furthermore, she speaks about the many sacrifices that her family has had to make in order to continue to get by.

Rachel

Rachel's parents are also married and she is an only child. She is a quiet girl who gets some of the best grades in her social studies class and excels in math and science. Rachel plays soccer and softball. Her usual school attire includes flared bottom jeans and knit shirts. She wears her long brown hair down and parted in the middle. Rachel tells me that her parents put a certain amount of pressure on her to get her homework done early and that she feels they have expectations for her. Here, Rachel talks about her father, who is a computer technician, and some of the things he tells her about going to college.

> **Rachel:** *Well my dad always says (laughing), 'I want you to go to school and get a really good job so you can pay for a nice college and so you can support us when we're old. You need to take care of us when we're old.' He's like, 'I'm putting all this money into your education so you can do well and everything.'*

Rachel also talks about the work her mother, who is a preschool teacher, does for Rachel and the family. Rachel discusses how she did not realize how difficult her mother's job was until she joined her at work one day.

> **Carrie:** *Do you have any role models, either in real life or the media?*
> **Rachel:** *My mom, because she's a teacher and she helped me to realize that teachers have a hard job. Because I went into her class—it wasn't easy for her. It's sort of like seeing, I don't know, I give her more credit for what she does. Plus, she does a lot of stuff for me at home. Like with laundry, to make sure I have clean clothes, you know.*

Rachel also talks about the multiple duties her mother takes on with both a full-time job and household chores. Hochschild has investigated the "second shift" that many working women with families endure. The "second shift" refers to the fact that numerous working women with male partners take on the majority of household chores because of established notions that the home is the woman's realm and household work, such as cooking, cleaning, and laundry, is women's work.[12] While Rachel acknowledges the second shift, her statement, unlike those of Maria, Amanda, and Alicia, takes on more of a tone of appreciation for her mother's work than a critique of her mother's workload or a desire to do things differently when she is older or a critique of gendered roles that have brought about this inequity.

Gwen

Gwen describes her mother as strong and determined. She tells me that her mother has worked hard all of her life to support herself and her two children. Her biological father left when Gwen was very young. Now remarried, Gwen's mother works at a donut shop where Gwen works with her after school. Gwen is a talkative girl with short blonde hair and a confident attitude. She describes herself as outspoken and brags that she is spoiled by her step-father who lets her drive his Cadillac to school and encourages her college and career plans. She does not invest herself in school-sanctioned extra-curricular activities and her closest friends go to other schools in the region. Gwen has arranged her schedule so that all of her classes are in the morning, and, on most days, she tries to leave school early to go to work or to work out. Here, Gwen speaks about her relationship with her mother.

> **Gwen:** *My mom taught me everything. She always tells me to be the best that I can be. She always tells me to reach for what I can, go for what I can. Do my, everything to the best of my ability. She's always taught me to be respectful, to be more mature. I'm more mature than I should be. She always teaches me everything that she never had. She tells me, she's like, 'I always want you to be better than I ever was,' stuff like that. She always compliments me, whatever. I really think that I was raised very well because my mom is, like, the best mom in the world. She worked eighty hours a week. She was a single mom for about nine years.*

Gwen tells me that her mother wants her to "be better" than she was and to have more in her life than she had. Both her mother, who works at the donut shop, and step-father, who works in a factory, encourage Gwen to attend college and become a lawyer. Gwen and her parents are invested in the idea that Gwen will educationally and economically surpass them.

Like many of the River City girls, Gwen is acutely aware of the struggles her family has endured and particularly sympathetic toward her mother. Her own future plans have developed within a family setting where she is encouraged to surpass the accomplishments of her parents educationally and financially.

As the only girl who I spoke with who intended to pursue a highly professional career path requiring graduate level education, Gwen's aspirations stood out. Yet, despite her educational and career goals, Gwen has detached herself from school and the school community. She does not participate in extra-curricular activities, does not socialize outside of school with River City students and has arranged a light schedule for herself which often allows her to leave school early. This disassociation in some ways seems contradictory to her goals of pursuing higher education and a professional career path. However, it can also be read as her desire to surpass the community's general educational expectations. Similarly, Fordham noted that African-American women, as a survival strategy in the academy, often distance themselves from their home culture in order to become part of the academic culture.[13] Gwen's behavior is in some ways similar to this as she focuses on the elements in her life, notably her parents, who share her goals for herself while disassociating with the school community which she may view as unsupportive.

In her work with white working-class women Weis notes that women, more often than men, are successful in their pursuit of higher education yet they remain entwined in the working-class culture because of their familiarity with it and their relationships within that culture.[14] At this point it remains unclear if Gwen is attempting to tear away from the working-class culture she wants to leave behind in terms of her educational and career choices. Her verbalization of her future plans seems to say this, however, her almost daily involvement with her after school job and the pride she takes in earning her paycheck and working her way up at the donut shop are reminiscent of the lads in Willis's work who claimed an adult status through their jobs while still in school which in turn led them directly into taking on these same sort of jobs as adults.[15]

Casey

Casey is a small girl with short, dirty-blonde hair. She dresses in baggy clothes and often wears jeans and a sweatshirt in dark colors. Casey struggles in school and has been diagnosed with a learning disability since arriving at River City High. Casey has experienced harsh, sometimes physically violent treatment from her father who she lived with in California until this school year when she moved in with her mother and step-father in River City. At River City, Casey skips classes a few times a week, and though she socializes with many students at River City, she describes herself as a loner and claims she has few friends.

Casey talks about growing up living with her father, who was in the military, and how the military lifestyle forced her mother to take on additional household responsibilities and created a situation where she felt she had to be "the good kid" so as not to put more stress on her already burdened mother. Unlike Maria, Amanda, and Gwen, Casey does not describe her mother as a strong woman. Instead, her mother's weakness and unsteadiness cause Casey to feel that she had to be the strong one in the relationship.

> *Casey: Well, my dad was military. He was a navy Seabee. [. . .] He retired when I was, like, nine years old. So, I mean, I've lived with the military for nine years of my life. So I'm used to it. I know how the family goes. Your dad goes away for six months; your mom has to be the pants wearer. You do anything, you bust your ass, you know. You have to be the good kid because mom is usually unsteady while dad's away. I'm used to the lifestyle.*

Like Rachel's mother, Casey's mother experienced a heavy domestic workload. Casey's mother took on traditionally male household roles when her father was away—she had, "to be the pants wearer" as well as being a mother and wife. As a result of her family's struggles, Casey felt forced to assume the responsibility for maintaining normalcy in her home. Unlike some of the other River City girls, Casey did not become closer with her mother as a result of a shared struggle. But Casey's situation is also different from the other girls'. She did not live with her mother after her parents divorced until last year when life with her father became unbearable, because of his alcoholism and violence, and she traveled across the country to live with her mother.

In some ways Casey seems caught in the cycles established by her parents. For example, when one of Casey's teachers called her home and informed her father that she was doing badly in class, Casey mimicked her father's violence toward her and threatened that teacher with a knife and found herself in jail by the next evening. In addition, although she discusses the stresses the military put on her family she also wants to join. Despite these familiar patterns Casey speaks candidly about mistakes she has made in her life and is optimistic about her River City High School experience.

As a group the River City girls, represented in part by Maria, Amanda, Alicia, Rachel, Gwen, and Casey reflect on their mother's lives as a way of informing their own future choices. They use their mothers' life histories as educational tools which are employed in the construction of their own gendered identities. The next section will discuss how some of the girls have adapted, or sometimes abandoned, their desires and dreams in order to live stable and settled lives.

Struggling Toward an Uncertain Future: The Desertion of Dreams

Many of the girls I interviewed have seen their mothers struggle with their educations, jobs, and/or marriages. Sociologists studying education have analyzed the ways in which adolescent girls position themselves for their futures in light of the school-based and family-based experiences that make up their adolescence. For example, McRobbie discusses the centrality of heterosexual romantic relationships and domestically-based work for the adolescent girls she studied.[16] Weis and Weiler look at the different ways that adolescent girls view their futures in light of a changed economic structure that could no longer promise working-class men a family wage that would allow their wives to stay at home and out of the paid workforce.[17] In the 1980s and 1990s, girls were talking more often about the importance of supporting themselves and having a career. For example, within the group of white working-class young women Weiler studied, she identifies three basic orientations toward the future: those who focus on family life as inevitable and only vaguely consider a career, those who consider family life as primary and have a secondary interest in a career, and those who are committed to careers.[18] She highlights the complexity of responses derived from one group of working-class young women. Weis reveals ways which white working-class adult women secure "settled lives" by contributing economically to their households (often pursuing higher education to do so) and forming relationships with men who work outside of the home but who also contribute to domestic work. Settled living, as opposed to hard living, includes those who have been able to, as families, earn enough money to provide a certain level of financial and resulting social stability. Weis takes the categories further by connecting them to gendered views of family life.

> Significantly, it is the movement off the space of white working-class hegemonic masculinity—that masculinity which emerged in relation to the old industrial economy—that now encourages this stability, since more "settled" jobs tend to be those associated with schooling (read, feminine in hegemonic parlance) and those traditionally coded as feminine (such as nurse, paralegal, hospital technician).[19]

Previous work on working-class women's lives helps to illustrate the complex ways that the traditional domestic ideology that is so central to McRobbie's work has been renegotiated as practical concerns about women being able to support themselves in uncertain times arise. As the girls from River City show, these uncertainties take many forms. Many of the girls (and boys) have seen their parents struggle economically as a result of divorce or loss of a job. In Alicia's case, her mother has not lost her job, but is fearful that she will if she does not take steps to make herself more desirable as an employee (in this case, that takes the form of higher education). Amanda is already feeling the pressure to provide for herself as she contemplates having to pay for her college education and possibly contribute to her family's income. While Gwen does not worry about paying for college, she still reflects on the struggles her family went through when her mother was a single parent.

Many River City girls plan for careers that they feel are their most practical option. Maria, whose mother is recently divorced, is acutely aware that her first career choice, being a dance instructor, is not a practical one that offers her necessities like health insurance. She has chosen to pursue a degree in psychology, a field she views as more practical. Chloe has a similar story.

Chloe

An athletic girl with shoulder-length blonde hair and a high-pitched voice, Chloe is friendly and giggled often during our interview. She plays lacrosse and participates in outdoor club and human rights club at the school. She also works at a coffee shop a few days a week. Chloe was an ice skater till a few years ago when it became too expensive for her family to finance what was becoming a more serious endeavor. She reflects on her skating days with some melancholy.

> *Carrie: So do you still skate at all, you gave it up entirely?*
> *Chloe: Yep [gave it up entirely].*
> *Carrie: Do you ever want to go back to it?*
> *Chloe: At times, yeah, because I'll see people I used to skate with or see it on TV and then I kind of miss it.*
> *Carrie: Was it a tough decision to give it up?*
> *Chloe: Yeah, because I did it for so long and, you know, that's why I was home schooled too, so . . . [Chloe was home schooled by her father, who is a nurse, through eighth grade]*
> *Carrie: Were you planning on doing it as a career?*
> *Chloe: Yeah, actually I was.*

Chloe describes the choice to give up skating as her own choice but one she was forced to make because her family lacked the financial resources to take her to the next level. She has now given it up entirely. Chloe's and Maria's cases are strikingly similar. Careers in skating and dancing do not materialize as realistic options for these young women. Coming from working-class backgrounds, the girls cannot afford the same choices that might be available to middle-class and certainly upper-class students. The pursuit of talent becomes secondary to economic stability. This is certainly not a solely working-class phenomenon, however the clash these girls experience between following their dreams and making practical career choices is highlighted in these stories. Guided by their parents Chloe and Maria each plan to go to college and pursue careers with more certainty and stability than skating and dancing.

The pressure to economically provide for oneself and one's family are repeated by many of the River City girls when discussing both their future plans and their mothers' stories. Divorce, the need for further education, and the threat of losing one's job are all stresses that call on these mothers and their daughters to be strong and stick together. The stories that the girls tell highlight the struggles created by family relationships, economic stress, loss of employment, and inadequate education as well as the necessity of strength. The girls discuss the fact that their mothers' struggles are both a part of their personal histories as well as lesson that inform their futures.

Though many of the girls are aware of the instability of both romantic relationships and employment, all continue to figure family into their future plans in different ways. Each of the girls I spoke with planned on having some sort of job or career in adulthood. Unlike in Weiler's study where she identifies a group of working-class girls who highlight family as primary, there were no River City girls who articulated this position. While most of them wanted a family, some of them talked about adjusting their career plans for the family, while others did not feel they would need to make any adjustment. Still, there was another group who was ambivalent about having children or did not want children at all. And Casey was the sole girl who told me she wanted two children and preferred to raise them on her own, without a partner.

Though these girls are negotiating new gendered roles for themselves, their expectations of men, outside of the idea that they cannot necessarily count on them, is little changed from previous generations of white working-class women. Generally, the girls do not talk about an expectation that men will contribute to domestic work and childcare specifically. This is a point Walkerdine et al. address in an exploration of working-class girls' identities. They point out the contradictory aspect of economic and social expectations.[20] Popular discourse tells girls that anything is possible, yet, at the same time, traditional gender expectations are imposed on them. In River City, the girls are encouraged to pursue careers, yet, at the same time, it is necessary for them to make provisions for children and domestic work which continues to be almost wholly a woman's responsibility.

In the next section, I discuss the past and present dating relationships of the girls of River City High School, how the girls reflect on romantic relationships, and the part these relationships may play in their perceptions of their futures.

Multiple Considerations: Career, Marriage and Children

The first section of this chapter touched on Maria's and Amanda's future plans. This section delves further into the future plans of some of the girls at River City High in terms of education, job, and family. Their mothers' life stories carry over into their discussions of future plans, and together with messages from school, work to shape their ideas of who they aspire to become.

Maria

Maria spoke about her desire to be a dance instructor and the competing need to have a stable income and health insurance. She also pointed to her mother's influence, both indirectly and directly pointing her toward a more stable career than dancing. Here, Maria talks more about her future.

> *Maria:* Ten years from now? In a house, married, hopefully. Being successful, doing my job, loving what I do. I want to, if I'm not in psychology hopefully I'll be doing something I love. I get up in the morning and I want to go to work. [. . .] Some people say it's selfish, but, like, if I want to get married, I want to be married for a sufficient amount of time to know that—I don't think you should throw kids in too fast, if you're not working on your relationship with your husband and you don't know what's going to happen or how stable. What if you got a divorce in two years and then you had kids? That would be my first fear, like, 'Oh my God' kind of thing. So, if I did, I'd give it a good five years so we could work out our stuff beforehand and not be shaky with kids thrown in there. Right now, I really don't want kids. I want to get, I want to do all this stuff, and if you have kids, you have to stop and have kids kind of thing. That's how I feel now, in ten years I might want five of them, you know. [laughs]

While Maria speaks about the importance of being happy in her job, she is also somewhat ambivalent about having children. First, she claims, "I don't want any kids." Next, she talks about the importance of developing a stable marriage before having children. She says, "So, if I did [have children], I'd give it a good five years so we could work out our stuff beforehand." Maria's awareness of the difficulty of marriage stands in contrast to the culture of romance that McRobbie and others have described in which girls look to marriage an achievement that will transport them away from the realities of providing for themselves and having to do well in school.[21] These sentiments are not Maria's alone: they are echoed by other girls who talk about the struggles of romantic relationships and the idea of wanting and needing to provide economically.

Amanda

Amanda talks about how her original plans to go to River City Community College were changed because her mother chose to move to Florida. Still interested in pursing a career where she can explore her vocal talent, Amanda talks about the disadvantages and difficulties of choosing a creative career, such as theater.

> *Amanda:* *In New York you either make it to Broadway or you don't make it to Broadway, but that's just the way it is. In New York, that's the main thing, you know, Erie's theater—it travels— so it's not even a theater company, it travels. Erie's theater travels everywhere, they have people coming into that theater in and out, in and out. Like, now, it's the* Full Monty, *it was the* Phantom of the Opera. *It's a traveling thing. I'm really not aiming towards that because I kind of want to get married when I'm older. But if I don't get married, I'm totally getting into that. It depends on what happens, you know, that's why I said I really don't have set plans.*

From Weiler's three basic future orientations displayed by the adolescent girls in her study Amanda best fits between two categories; one in which the girls consider family life as primary and have a secondary interest in a career, and the other in which girls are committed to careers and view family life as secondary.[22] While Amanda focuses on her future career as primary, she also realizes that traveling with a show might make a marriage difficult.

Unlike Amanda, Chloe does not articulate a need to alter her current career plans in order to have a family.

Chloe

Chloe, who was preparing to be a professional ice skater until it became too financially strenuous for her family, is now considering fashion design.

> *Carrie:* *Where do you picture yourself five years from now?*
> *Chloe:* *Five years from now?*
> *Carrie:* *So if you went to college, you'd probably be finishing up your senior year.*
> *Chloe:* *I can just picture myself in New York designing for some company and living in a small apartment in Manhattan or something, you know.*
> *Carrie:* *What about ten years from now?*
> *Chloe:* *Ten years from now? I'd probably move outside of New York a little bit and probably have a family, hopefully, be married.*
> *Carrie:* *Do you want kids or have you thought about that?*
> *Chloe:* *Yeah, I want at least two, a maximum of three.*

Chloe's future plans combine both career and family. She envisions a stage in her life where she is a single career woman and a later stage in which she moves out of the city and raises children.

Gwen

Gwen, who wants to be a lawyer or a judge, talks about her future plans for marriage and a family. She reflects on the uncertainty of the future and the idea that things may not turn out as she best imagines them.

> *Carrie: Where do you picture yourself five years from now? [. . .]*
> *Gwen: I'd probably be going into law school or I'd be a freshman in law school. Probably getting married. Probably having kids, starting a family. That's where I picture myself when I'm twenty five. Not going to happen, but . . .*
> *Carrie: How many kids do you want?*
> *Gwen: Two, that's it, just two.*
> *Carrie: Why do say it's not going to happen?*
> *Gwen: Because. It's just, it's not. Everything you want to happen, if you don't work for it, I mean you cannot work for finding a husband, getting married, everything by twenty five. It's just, it doesn't work out that way. You have to let it flow.*

Gwen, who would fit Weiler's category of being committed to a career first, does not envision having to sacrifice her career aspirations in order to have a marriage and family. She talks about having two children and has even chosen names for them.

Rachel

Unlike Chloe and Gwen, who answer my questions about where they view themselves in five and ten years with some certainty, having already given the subject thought, Rachel stumbles over the idea of considering herself at twenty two and twenty seven years old.

> *Carrie: Where do you picture yourself five years from now?*
> *Rachel: Hopefully, with a job. Hopefully, I won't still be in school. If I am still in school, it's okay but hopefully I'll be in a job and starting my career.*
> *Carrie: Any particular location or place in the country you want to be?*
> *Rachel: No. I haven't thought that far ahead.*
> *Carrie: Well this question is going to be really hard then. Where do you picture yourself ten years from now?*
> *Rachel: [laughs] I don't know, I don't know. Probably a little bit more settled into my job. Move out on my own, maybe have an apartment of my own. An apartment of my own, probably not a house. I don't think I'll be that independent. I'll probably still be close to my parents. Probably still in the area.*

[. . .]
Carrie: *What about as far as the ten years from now, do you picture yourself as married or anything like that?*
Rachel: *Probably not. [laughs] No. I don't know. I could be, but I
don't know. It seems so far away to think that I'll be married in ten
years, you know.*

Rachel does not dismiss marriage outright, as Casey did, but she finds it virtually
impossible to envision that far ahead into her future right now.

While the girls at River City High articulate a variety of career options for themselves, not one adheres strictly to the orientation (from Weiler's three orientations)
that focuses on family life as inevitable and only vaguely considers a career. Many of
the girls assumed they would have a marriage and/or a family at some point in their
lives. Few of them expressed that their own career would be either secondary or
temporary, in fact, quite the contrary. Having a family necessitates also having a job
in order to provide for oneself and one's children. However, the girls did acknowledge that getting married and having children would necessitate a lifestyle change of
some sort. For example, Chloe and Gwen both talk about moving out of the city in
order to raise children. Amanda expressed that she might rule out a career that involved extensive travel in order to accommodate a marriage, yet her desire to pursue
a career in performance was still strong despite economic considerations. Again,
these girls are juggling some of the competing expectations they feel, the need to
both have a career and fulfill traditional roles of wife and mother in ways that sometimes contradict with each other, a contradiction these girls have been made more
aware of through their mother's lives and struggles.

Conclusion

The girls at River City High School speak about their future plans as stemming from
their personal and family histories, their educational experiences, and their hopes and
dreams. As they prepare for their futures, the girls are placing themselves in a position to redefine gender roles as they conceptualize the role of women as necessarily
self-sufficient. The girls discuss the trials and tribulations of life, the struggles of
their mothers, and their personal realizations that they will have to be practical about
their own futures if they plan to get themselves through life's struggles.

Studies of adolescent girls often attest to the lack of communication and distance
between white girls and their mothers and the ways these distances impact the girls
psychologically, going hand-in-hand with low self-esteem and a variety of related
issues.[23] However, my work with the River City girls contradicts these conclusions
and illustrates the ways the girls' identities were entwined with their relationships
with their mothers. Not only do the River city girls identify with their mothers in
terms of their personal histories and life stories but many of them also had close
relationships with their mothers and valued their approval and trust. The relationships, shared family responsibilities, and struggles of the River City girls are more

reminiscent of the African-American girls' relationships with their mothers who often shared responsibilities such as childrearing[24] and African-American mothers who worked to teach their daughters life-lessons as a way of protecting them from the harsh realities of racism.[25] In the case of the white working-class mothers the life-lessons function not to protect against racism but against economic and gender based struggles.

Though the River City girls and their mothers share their knowledge and wisdom about life's struggles, they view these struggles as generally personal rather than class-based. While the girls appear to understand these struggles, at least somewhat, in terms of their gender, they stop short of reaching a class-based understanding of them. Although these struggles are articulated closely with gender roles and issues that impact women, the girls have also not opened up a dialogue of expressing gender solidarity. The discussion of "being a team" and sharing struggles is most often talked about in terms of a family struggle and, more specifically, a mother and daughter struggle but rarely expanded to include other women.

As Weis notes, working-class women have often not identified with the women's movement, but they do use the language of the movement in their articulations around their gendered identities.[26] This is strikingly similar to what the River City girls are doing. Maria and Amanda, for example, speak the language of gender solidarity, yet fail to conceptualize their gender-based struggles as ones that extend outside of their personal family dynamic.

While many of the girls have ambitious hopes for their futures, they are acutely aware that life does not offer them guarantees. Gwen, Maria, Amanda, Alicia and Casey have already thought about sacrifices they might make in the future. And Chloe has already made one such sacrifice, giving up her skating career because it became too expensive for her to become a professional.

The girls at River City High discuss the ways the school and home cultures that they are a part of play roles in their ideas about their futures and the roles they will take on in the future. Gender is being reconceptualized by the girls in new ways and, at the same time, they are also discussing careers, some of which step outside of what are generally though of as working-class jobs because of the level of education they require. The economic changes that have often altered their parents' lives have encouraged these adolescents to find a new niche in a changing economy. Quite a few of the careers the students are aiming for require at least some college education, which brings to mind questions about whether or not these students have been given the educational and cultural capital to succeed in college.

The next chapter looks at the River City boys and the ways their ideas about their futures compare with those of the girls.

Notes

1. McRobbie, A. "Working Class Girls and the Culture of Femininity." In *Women Take Issue: Aspects of Women's Subordination*, edited by CCCS. London: Hutchinson, 1978; Hol-

land, D., and M. Eisenhart. *Educated in Romance: Women, Achievement, and College Culture.* Chicago: University of Chicago Press, 1990.

2. Gaskell, J. *Gender Matters: From School to Work.* Philadelphia: Open University Press, 1992.

3. Gaskell, J. "Gender and Course Choice: The Orientation of Male and Female Students." *Journal of Education* 166 (1984): 89-102.

4. Orenstein, P. *Schoolgirls: Young Women, Self-Esteem, and the Confidence Gap.* New York: Anchor Books, 1995.

5. McRobbie, A. "Working Class Girls and the Culture of Femininity." In *Women Take Issue: Aspects of Women's Subordination,* edited by CCCS. London: Hutchinson, 1978; Weiler, J.D. *Codes and Contradictions: Race, Gender Identity, and Schooling.* Albany: SUNY Press, 2000; Proweller, A. *Constructing Identities: Meaning Making in an Upper Middle Class Youth Culture.* New York: State University of New York Press, 1998.

6. McRobbie, A. "Working Class Girls and the Culture of Femininity." In *Women Take Issue: Aspects of Women's Subordination,* edited by CCCS. London: Hutchinson, 1978; Willis, P. *Learning to Labor: How Working Class Kids Get Working Class Jobs.* New York: Columbia University Press, 1977.

7. Weiler, J.D. *Codes and Contradictions: Race, Gender Identity, and Schooling.* Albany: SUNY Press, 2000.

8. Proweller, A. *Constructing Identities: Meaning Making in an Upper Middle Class Youth Culture.* New York: State University of New York Press, 1998.

9. Holland, D., and M. Eisenhart. *Educated in Romance: Women, Achievement, and College Culture.* Chicago: University of Chicago Press, 1990.

10. Millls, R., and S. Bhandari. "Health Insurance Coverage in the United States: 2002." edited by Economics and Statistics Administration U.S. Department of Commerce: U.S. Census Bureau, 2003.

11. Bloom, J. "Hollowing the Promise of Higher Education: Inside the Political Economy of Access to College." In *Beyond Silenced Voices: Class, Race and Gender in United States Schools,* edited by L. Weis and M. Fine. Albany: SUNY Press, 2005.

12. Hochschild, A. *The Second Shift.* New York: Penguin Books, 2003.

13. Fordham, S. "'Those Loud Black Girls' (Black) Women, Silence, and 'Gender Passing' in the Academy." In *Beyond Black and White: New Faces and Voices in U.S. Schools,* edited by M. Seller and L. Weis. Albany: SUNY Press, 1997.

14. Weis, L. *Class Reunion: The Remaking of the American White Working Class.* New York: Routledge, 2004.

15. Willis, P. *Learning to Labor: How Working Class Kids Get Working Class Jobs.* New York: Columbia University Press, 1977.

16. McRobbie, A. "Working Class Girls and the Culture of Femininity." In *Women Take Issue: Aspects of Women's Subordination,* edited by CCCS. London: Hutchinson, 1978.

17. Weis, L. *Working Class without Work: High School Students in a Deindustrializing Economy.* New York: Routledge, 1990; Weiler, J.D. *Codes and Contradictions: Race, Gender Identity, and Schooling.* Albany: SUNY Press, 2000.

18. Weiler, J.D. *Codes and Contradictions: Race, Gender Identity, and Schooling.* Albany: SUNY Press, 2000.

19. Weis, L. *Class Reunion: The Remaking of the American White Working Class.* New York: Routledge, 2004. 90.

20. Walkerdine, V., H. Lucey, and J. Melody. "Growing up Girl: Psychological Explorations of Gender and Class." In *Off White: Readings on Power, Privilege and Resistance,* edited by M. Fine, L. Weis, P. Pruitt and A. Burns. New York: Routledge, 2004.

21. McRobbie, A. "Working Class Girls and the Culture of Femininity." In *Women Take*

Issue: Aspects of Women's Subordination, edited by CCCS. London: Hutchinson, 1978; Holland, D., and M. Eisenhart. *Educated in Romance: Women, Achievement, and College Culture.* Chicago: University of Chicago Press, 1990.

22. Weiler, J.D. *Codes and Contradictions: Race, Gender Identity, and Schooling.* Albany: SUNY Press, 2000.

23. Gaines, D. *Teenage Wasteland: Suburbia's Dead End Kids.* Chicago: University of Chicago Press, 1998; Kenny, L. D. *Daughters of Suburbia: Growing up White, Middle Class, and Female.* New Brunswick: Rutgers University Press, 2000; Orenstein, P. *Schoolgirls: Young Women, Self-Esteem, and the Confidence Gap.* New York: Anchor Books, 1995; Pipher, M. *Reviving Ophelia: Saving the Selves of Adolescent Girls.* New York: Ballatine Books, 1994.

24. Orenstein, P. *Schoolgirls: Young Women, Self-Esteem, and the Confidence Gap.* New York: Anchor Books, 1995.

25. Fordham, S. "'Those Loud Black Girls' (Black) Women, Silence, and 'Gender Passing' in the Academy." In *Beyond Black and White: New Faces and Voices in U.S. Schools*, edited by M. Seller and L. Weis. Albany: SUNY Press, 1997.

26. Weis, L. *Class Reunion: The Remaking of the American White Working Class.* New York: Routledge, 2004.

Chapter Three

Boys at River City High School

They're [my parents] pretty happy that my grades are good considering how both of them dropped out and had to come here for their GEDs.

Doug—age seventeen

While both the boys and girls come from relatively the same places economically River City boys' and girls' stories were both similar and different in some striking ways. For example, they articulate their future plans in different ways. The girls speak of strength and lessons learned from the struggles of those around them, their mothers in particular, while the boys are not so articulate about these struggles. Instead the boys' dialogue focuses on choices, in terms of what they will do educationally, career-wise, where they will live, and so on. Most of the boys plan to attend college (only one boy in the group did not), yet there is an overall concern about the expense of higher education and how they will pay for their education.

When comparing these new century working-class boys to Willis's lads, there are also differences and similarities. The drastically changed economy has effectively removed the promise of a factory job that the lads in Willis's *Learning to Labor* transitioned into immediately after high school. Instead, the River City boys face an economy in which a "decent" job, one that will allow them to have a house, car, and family (though not necessarily support all of these single-handedly) most likely requires a college education.[1] Many of the parents of River City students have learned this lesson the hard way. Alicia's mother, from the last chapter, went back to school, not in order to move up, but in hopes of retaining her secretarial job as her company moved many of its jobs overseas.

The struggles that the girls discuss are unique to their gender and not shared by the River City boys. Only three boys discuss the struggles of their mothers; two of these boys also talk about fathers who are prevented from working by injuries or disabilities they suffered recently. Unlike the previous generations of white working-class boys this generation of River City boys does not consider their futures in relation to the loss of unionized jobs.[2] Though the boys appear to be aware of the struggles their parents face with respect to education, employment, and family, they do not focus on these struggles in the same way as the girls. Most importantly, they do not share them or internalize them in the form of stories that inform their own identities and outlook on their futures, the way the girls do. Almost all of the girls in this group identified "life lessons" from their family histories. Two of their common conclusions are: that a college education is a necessity to get a job that supports their needs/families, and that their futures, especially when it comes to career and family, are uncertain, which further adds to the need for a college education and the stability and earning power that are equated with that education. The girls directly apply these "life lessons" to their own ideas about who they are and who they want to become.

Though the boys have witnessed the same struggles, they stop short of personalizing them or connecting them directly to their own futures. The boys acknowledge the need for a college education; though instead of framing it as a necessity, as the girls do, they discuss it in terms of personal opportunity. They focus on the ways their interests and aptitudes have led them to pursue certain occupations, many of which require post-secondary education. This represents a victory for neoliberal ideas about higher education as an opportunity which stresses personal accomplishment, individual achievement, and educational consumerism.

The boys rarely talk about a need for financial or emotional independence as a reason to pursue higher education or a career. The differences in the girls' and boys' articulations of necessity versus opportunity raise questions about the ways the girls and boys understand their future class and gender roles. These differences raise questions about whether the boys and girls are creating meanings from events differently or communicating their concerns in different ways. To help clarify this, I begin by exploring the ways the boys talk about family struggle in the few cases where it was acknowledged.

Taking Care of Family

Girls from River City shared detailed stories about the struggles of their mothers, but the boys did not as often refer to their mothers' challenges. In fact, there were only two boys who related stories about their mothers' struggles with family, education, and employment. Brian and Lloyd talk about how hard their mothers work to support their families.

Brian

Brian is a sixteen-year-old junior and an avid soccer player. Brian has blonde, short hair and he wears glasses. He and his girlfriend, Mia, who also plays soccer, have been together for over a year and Brian's social life revolves around their relationship. His interview with me was dominated by stories about his girlfriend and his mother. When he talks about his father, it is only to critique him for not taking care of his family.

> *Carrie: So, what family members do you live with right now?*
> *Brian: I live with my mom, my sisters, my two brothers. We have no contact with my dad. [. . .] It's the whole thing, like one time he came in and decided to give us hugs or something, for no reason, in a weird way. He's a horrible father and everything like*

that, and he wasn't there for us. But my mom, she's a really, really hard worker. She works four [he exaggerates here but later confirms she works two jobs, maybe three] jobs, she takes care of four children. My mom, she gets up, she takes us to school, then she goes to her school. [. . .] She's a pre-K teacher. And she takes care of that. She leaves at four, but she stays there till five thirty because there's an after school program there. And then she works at Big Shop, she works with me, that's kind of cool. [. . .]

Carrie: Did she go to college at all?

Brian: She went to, my dad didn't want her to go to college—he went to college and then he quit. It was the whole thing like that; he wouldn't go because he went golfing or something like that. So my mom, she's, like, hesitant about it, you know. She still works and everything. [. . .] She tries so hard. You have to give respect to people, and she's always nice to everybody. Everything's so great, like how she does things. I see that she had to get everything. No matter what, she tries so hard. She had to go all out. Work at Big Shop on the weekends from like six in the morning till two.

Brian shows great concern and involvement with his mother's struggles with her education, career, and providing for her family. He tells me that his father "didn't want her to go to college." Now, she works as a preschool teacher during the week and at a discount store on weekends. Brian tells me that, because of her dedication, perseverance, and hard work, he sees his mother as a role model.

Lloyd

Lloyd is a quiet boy in class but opened up one-on-one. He plays baseball outside of school and wants to try out for boys' volleyball when the school starts a team next year. Lloyd is a large boy who often wears a hockey jersey or other sports-oriented clothing. Lloyd's siblings are much older than him, in their thirties and forties. He has few friends at River City High School; most of his friends are younger and attend middle school in a different building. Lloyd's mother is the sole breadwinner in his family. Here, he talks about how hard his mother, who is sixty years old, works to support the family.

Carrie: Who do you live with right now?

Lloyd: My parents.

Carrie: Just your parents?

Lloyd: Um, hum [yes].

Carrie: And was your dad always handicapped or did he injure himself?

Lloyd: No, what happened is he has diabetes. He used to work at Convenient Mart and one day, he was getting, I don't know how

that happened—he had hip problems. They had to put an artificial hip in him. And then after that, one day, when I was in middle school, I don't know what grade it was, the one day he woke up and his toes on one of his feet was all purple. So, they rushed him to the hospital and they had to amputate them. That was the only option and that's how it's been.
Carrie: So, your mom works a lot then?
Lloyd: Yeah. She has two jobs.
Carrie: What does she do?
Lloyd: She's a home health care aide for, I can't think of the company right now, it's on Elm in Norburg. And she also works at Super-Market. She works in the deli at Super-Market.
Carrie: Does she like her jobs?
Lloyd: She'd like to get away. She'd like to only work one, but they won't give her the full-time at Super-Market. But she gets a lot of benefits at Super-Market, that's why she likes that job.
[. . .] Carrie: Did they [your parents] go to college or graduate from high school?
Lloyd: She tried to go to college but then, I guess, I don't know. Something didn't work out. My dad never did. He said he wishes he would have.

Like Brian's mother, Lloyd's mother tried to attend college. Lloyd tells me, "Something didn't work out." Lloyd's father also did not attend college and now, unable to work due to his hip replacement and amputations, he wishes he would have.

When the River City girls recounted the stories of their mothers' struggles, they used them to illustrate the lessons they had learned and related these lessons to their future plans and expectations. The boys, however, did not take that step to connect their mothers' struggles to life lessons or associate them with their future plans. Instead the boys positioned themselves outside of the stories.

White working-class adolescent boys studied by Willis and Weis have clung to a traditional version of hegemonic masculinity. Willis's lads embrace a masculinity that is strongly aligned with manual labor and in opposition to authority. The lads further define themselves in opposition to the feminine and racial "others" which make up their community and school. The white working-class boys in Weis's study adopt a similar form of masculinity. They echo opposition to authority as well as racial and feminine "others."[3] However, these boys are not as ardently opposed to higher education, which Willis's lads define as feminine.

Traditional white working-class hegemonic masculinity, along with a manual labor occupation, in the past allowed working-class men not only to occupy the role of economic provider but also allowed them to form an identity in opposition to mental labor, which is coded as feminine.[4] In the absence of decently paid and readily available manual labor jobs the boys of River City no longer have the option of constructing a masculinity that follows this traditional working-class model. The boys I spoke with look to mental labor or skilled labor, usually requiring a college credential. It is important to point out that even these new jobs requiring higher education will most likely not provide enough income for men to be sole breadwinners for a family. In light of this, new articulations of masculinity are formed that incorporate a new world view, which includes men doing mental labor and not being the sole breadwinner. However, like the girls, the boys also struggle to balance traditional expectations and developing economic and social realities. The next section explores one of the ways some of the boys reinterpret gender roles in light of a new social reality.

The Role of Protector

Brian, Lloyd, and Dan all have mothers who are breadwinners for the family. While other boys from River City mentioned their mothers' jobs, they did not generally express how their mothers felt about their jobs or what difficulties they faced in their lives. However, their lack of attention to these struggles does not mean that they do not exist, only that they were unacknowledged by the boys or not focused on in the same ways the girls highlighted them.

The girls speak about their mothers' challenges as life lessons from which they are learning. The boys who acknowledge their mothers' struggles express sympathy for their mothers, but did not draw connections between their mothers' struggles and their own future plans. In Dan's case, for example, he places himself in the role of a care taker for his newborn brother or sister.

Dan

Dan is a popular boy who talks and jokes often during class. He is tall and muscular and wears his dirty-blonde hair in a short buzz cut. He plays football and hopes to be awarded a football scholarship for college. Although Dan's dreams are big, his teachers are critical of him. Two of his teachers expressed concern about his failing grades and additional concern about the growing reality that he would be kicked off of the football team if his grades and attitude did not improve. Dan's mother and father have been separated for two years, and his mother is pregnant with her live-in boyfriend's child. Dan talks about how he wants to help out with the baby when it comes.

> *Dan: I want a study hall first period [next year] because my mom's pregnant—she's about to have a baby in, like, three weeks. [. . .] because she works nights, so if she had to stay after work for one day, I could stay home first period so I wouldn't have to come to school. I talked to Mr. Ferell [the guidance counselor] about it and he said he'd try to give me a first period study hall.*

Dan's response when I ask about his parents' jobs reveals that while he is familiar with the details of his father's job, he is not so familiar with his mother's work.

> **Dan:** *My dad is an apartment manager, he manages sixty units, a big complex. And my mom, I'm not sure what she does. I know she works nights. I think she helps build the inside of cars, like the dashboard and then she helps make the plastic.*
> **Carrie:** *Do they like their jobs?*
> **Dan:** *My dad does. I don't know. I think my mom's job, wasn't, the fact that it's nights, if it was during the day, I think she would like it more, but she doesn't really like it that much, I don't think.*

Dan avoids talking much about his mother's live-in boyfriend or any ways that he contributes to the household or plans to contribute when the baby arrives; instead, Dan focuses on his own role.

Brian and Lloyd highlight their mothers' roles as care takers of the family, both economically and emotionally. Each of these boys tells me the reasons their fathers are not in traditional roles of provider or caretaker. In Brian's case, he calls his father a "horrible father" and even cites his father as the reason his mother did not go to college—"my dad didn't want her to go to college"—thereby contributing to her struggle today. Lloyd's father worked up until a few years ago when he encountered health problems and as a result cannot work now. His mother works two jobs, providing for her family. Dan, whose father also had to leave his job as a result of a disability and now manages an apartment complex, talks about how he would like to step in to take care of his family, not as a breadwinner, but as a caregiver.

These three boys, like many of the girls, recognize their mothers' struggles. However, instead of identifying with or internalizing them the way the girls do the boys each express some desire to protect or care for their mothers. The role of protector is a more socially acceptable role for a male than the more empathetic role the girls play in relation to their struggling mothers and follows the path of a traditional version of masculinity. However, the traditional white working-class hegemonic version of masculinity does not fit into a new world in which many of these boys find themselves talking about going to college, pursuing mental labor, and being raised by their single mothers. Mac an Ghaill and Imms argue that a complex definition is needed in order to understand masculinity in its multiple forms.[5] Imms writes,

> contemporary masculinity discourses have largely failed by constructing images of masculinity that are removed from men's actual practices. Hegemonic patriarchal theory is effective for explaining the oppressed status of women, and men "on the street" may perhaps acknowledge hegemony over women in theory. But few would agree that they live it. This makes the theory difficult to use in ethnographic research because it diverges from participants' perceptions.[6]

The masculinities expressed by the River City boys are likewise complex. Like the girls who struggle with traditional gender roles, new demands, and dreams, the boys also find themselves in a place where new gender identities must be created in light of new economic and social realities and lived realities, by necessity, can differ from stated concepts of gender roles. In these cases where the boys acknowledge the struggles of their mothers, they also rely on more traditional models of masculinity which stress the need for a male to be a provider, and if not a provider, at least a protector. The traditional role clashes with the reality; that there is no male provider.

Future Plans: College

All except one of the boys interviewed plan to go to college after high school. Like many of the girls, some of the boys express the desire to stay near home and attend either the local community college or another local school. At the height of industrialization, working-class young men expected to find work after high school in the manufacturing industry, as their fathers had.[7] These manufacturing jobs paid well, offered benefits, and did not require post-secondary education. Men expected that they could support their families on their wages, without requiring their wives to work. This is no longer the case in River City and most of the country, and thus River City boys look toward higher education.

Literature on white working-class adolescent boys has focused on the changing definitions of the working class from a group defined by its work and the place of that work in the economy to a more comprehensive definition that considers cultural as well as economic factors.[8] The definition of class employed here also extends past a group's relationship to the means of production and focuses on group identities that are defined by and define a group's relationship with society and its cultural hierarchy, with emphasis on money, occupation, opportunity, and education.

Willis stresses that the working-class culture "knows" the economic reality of the job market. Part of this knowing involves understanding the reality of what the job market has to offer and what is needed, or not needed, to obtain a working-class job.[9] I argue that there is a similar group understanding of the job market operating among the working-class adolescents at River City High School. Though this knowledge is articulated in different ways, particularly by the boys and the girls, there is a new understanding that a college education is necessary in order to obtain a decent job. Without some level of college education there is a realization that the job market will have little to offer other than low-level service and retail jobs.

Willis's lads from the 1970s do not experience this due to the fact that at this time factory jobs were abundant. However, in a later investigation of working class adolescents Weis finds that "40 percent express a desire to go to a two- or four-year college, and there is far less celebration of manual-laboring jobs than earlier studies suggest."[10] This study, in many ways following up on Weis's, finds the majority of adolescents expressing not only a desire, but a necessity, to attend college.

The majority of River City students wants to, and plan to, go to college. Despite this, most of the students who spoke with me in the second half of their junior year were unfamiliar with the college application process, the college and university hierarchy, and availability of financial aid. Though guidance counselors are available for help, the organized college night at River City was open to only the first two hundred students to sign up. With approximately 400 juniors at the school, the list filled up quickly. In addition, the outstanding question remains about how well these River City students will fare in a college environment.

River City students talked about the importance of a college education in terms of a credential as opposed to a life experience or learning experience. The conversations that follow reveal how these young, white, working-class males are focusing on college. None of the boys who spoke with me expressed any expectations of getting manufacturing or factory jobs after high school, and all but one of the boys who spoke with me envisioned attending college after high school.

Bob, Joseph, and Mike all plan on going to two-year schools for trades such as auto body, auto technician, and welding. Brian and Aaron both want to be physical education teachers. Lloyd would like to either become an umpire or a state trooper. Each of these occupations require a physical, hands-on component reminiscent of, but not the same as, the working-class respect and valorization of manual labor which Willis analyzes. Willis explains that in the lads' working-class culture, manual labor becomes equated with masculinity: "Thus physical laboring comes to stand for and express, most importantly, a kind of masculinity and also an opposition to authority—at least as it is learned in school."[11] Although some River City boys have chosen occupations which include aspects of manual or physical labor reminiscent of the lads, the River City boys do not share the lads' fierce opposition to authority. Instead, they acknowledge, at least in words, the value of education to prepare them for future jobs and also to provide them with a life experience.

While the girls also talked about going to college, girls and boys articulate the necessity for a college education very differently and the girls expressed different motivations from the boys'. The girls were vocal about the struggles they had seen or experienced and the need for a college education to buffer them from experiencing some of the struggles their mothers had endured and they focused on necessity and reality when choosing a future career. For the boys, however, the idea of a college education is expressed as an opportunity and a choice. While the working-class culture might "know" the necessity of a college education, the boys' individual articulations of this do not include words of necessity or family stories of economic need and struggle. A few of the boys also expressed pride at being the first in their families to have this opportunity.

This articulation is further complicated by the idea that earning a college degree, while it may move the boys up in terms of educational attainment, compared to past generations of working-class men, it will not necessarily move them up in terms of their place in the class-based economic hierarchy or even how much money they will make.

Most of the River City boys who spoke with me come from families where their parents either never attended, or did not finish, college. Out of the fourteen boys I interviewed, a total of seven of their parents/step-parents/guardians had completed either a two or four year college degree (this includes any adult having or at one time having taken a parental role for each student). Quite a few of these boys are the first generation in their families to attend college.

Bob

Bob is a quiet boy in school who often falls asleep during his eighth period social studies class. He has short, brown hair and often hides his face under the hood of a sweatshirt. More than one of his teachers suspects he is a drug user. Bob had difficulties living with his mother and her new husband, so he recently moved in with his grandparents who live in River City. Bob, whose grandfather graduated from college, tells me that he is the oldest and first grandchild who plans to attend college.

> *Carrie: Do your parents ever give you advice about school or anything like that?*
> *Bob: Advice about college?*
> *Carrie: Just in general, about either college or high school.*
> *Bob: Not really. I think I'm the only one that's ever gone.*
> *Carrie: Oh really, in your whole family?*
> *Bob: No, my mom went for a little while. I forget what she was going for but she just quit. I don't think anybody else ever went. My grandfather went. I think he went for business or something like that, but, like, I'm the oldest grandchild out of all my grandparents' kids. I'm the only one who is going to college, so.*

While Bob talks about his plans to attend college, his current academic performance raises questions about what colleges he might be able to attend, as well as how well he will be able to do in college. Observing Bob in his social studies class, he spends much of the class period with his head down on his desk, sometimes asleep. Generally, he does not engage with the class lessons, and one of his teachers, Mrs. Carson, made negative comments regarding his performance in class.

Joseph

Joseph, a football player, is well known in school for his accomplishments on the field. He is a large boy with dark, curly hair and prides himself on his Italian heritage. Joseph tells me that his mother dropped out of high school, and his father dropped out of college when his brother was born.

> *Carrie: What do they tell you about school?*
> *Joseph: Work hard, don't be like them.*
> *Carrie: Don't be like them, why?*
> *Joseph: Well, my mom dropped out and my dad had my older brother, so he never got to finish college.*
> *Carrie: OK. So he was in college when your brother was born?*
> *Joseph: Yeah.*
> *Carrie: And do they want you to go to college?*
> *Joseph: Yeah.*

Joseph says that his parents advise him, "Don't be like them." His parents would like to see him graduate from college and exceed their own educational levels.

Doug

Doug is a popular football player who is also a class clown, attracting the attention of his teachers and fellow students. Doug wears small, wire-rimmed glasses and dresses, like most of the boys, in jeans and a t-shirt almost every day. Though Doug's grades are quite good and he tells me many of his classes interest him, his classroom persona presents the opposite image. When Doug is not making jokes, he often puts his head down on his desk and appears to be tuning out. Both of Doug's parents dropped out of high school and earned their GEDs.

> *Carrie: What do your parents tell you about school?*
> *Doug: They're pretty happy that my grades are good considering how both of them dropped out and had to come here for their GEDs.*
> *Carrie: Did either of them go to college?*
> *Doug: Nope. They're pretty psyched about that too [Doug going to college].*

Like many of the River City students, Doug plans to be the first generation in his family to attend college. Already he is surpassing his parents' educational accomplishments by staying in high school and working toward graduation.

Benjamin

Benjamin plays ice hockey for the high school. He has short, brown hair and often sits in the back of the class. He was in honor society until recently when his average dropped too low for him to participate. Both of Benjamin's parents graduated from local colleges. Here, he talks about his college plans and his parents' desire that he stay near home.

> *Carrie: What do your parents tell you about school?*
> *Benjamin: They're pretty strict about it. They want me to study and do good. They always tell me it definitely plays a huge factor in what my future's going to be in. I should want to do good. They're not going to force me to do work if I don't want to. It's my own future but they're pretty hard on me. They tell me to study all the time. I listen to them—I mean, I want to do good in school. I'm not going to blow anything off.*
> *[. . .] Carrie: OK. What do you plan to do when you graduate from high school?*

Benjamin: *I'm looking to go to college. I'm looking at State University and Waterville and St. Damian because I don't think I'm allowed to go out of, like, too far away. Like I was looking at Hillside State, too and I like it there, but I don't know if I want to go that far or not. I just, I don't know [. . .] Me and my parents have been talking about that. I'm most likely going to live at home, at least for the first two years of college. We were talking about how we could turn the basement into a bigger room for me, and I could get my computer down there and so I could live at home.*

Deciding whether or not to leave home or leave the area for college is something many of the boys talk about. Though the majority of these interviews were done near the end of the boys' junior years, many of them were still indecisive about what their plans were.

Joseph

Joseph, the football player, is a large boy whose family moved to River City six years ago from a nearby city. His father works for a neighboring county and his mother works at the school attached to his family's church. Here, Joseph explains his own plans and the plans of many of his friends.

Carrie: *How do you think that your plans are the same or different from your friends'?*
Joseph: *They all want to go into something else. I'll stick with mine [Joseph wants to go to a two-year school for auto body work]. And my friends want to go somewhere else but I think they might be back [. . .] Some of them want to go to North State or all those other schools. Most of them are going to RCCC though [laughs].*
Carrie: *So they want to go to other schools but you think they're going to end up at RCCC?*
Joseph: *Yeah.*

Joseph expresses his belief that most of his friends will end up going to the local community college even though they want to go to other regional schools. He tells me, laughing, "Most of them are going to RCCC, though." Many of the boys and girls discuss feeling both financial and emotional pressures to stay at home, or at the very least, near home, after high school. River City Community College or RCCC is a school of approximately five thousand students and is a ten minute drive from the high school. All of the vocational training center classes are held either on the campus or next door at the VTC's own building. The students at River City are familiar with River City Community College and its campus. Even those who do not attend VTC at the campus occasionally visit for school events, such as a local college fair, which is held there. Many also have friends who graduated and attend school there.

One of the high school's guidance counselors, Mr. Ferell, frequently mentions RCCC to his students. When he visited social studies classes to talk to eleventh graders about post-high school plans, he presented the students' options as four: work, military, RCCC, or another college. The students who would like a four-year degree are also encouraged to consider attending RCCC for two years and then transferring into a four-year school as a money-saving option, as well as a way to boost their grades before transferring. The four regional schools mentioned most frequently by River City students range in cost from $2,976 a year for tuition at the local community college to $17,700 for tuition at a local private university. The two nearby state schools both charge $4,350 per year for in-state residents. When comparing the annual tuition, room, and board package at Waterville U (the local private university) which is $26,470 with RCCC at $2,976 (no room and board available), it becomes very clear why so many working-class students attend RCCC.

In addition to being financially practical, River City Community College is familiar and comfortable to the students. As mentioned, many have some experience with the college before they graduate either through visiting, taking vocational classes which are held on the RCCC campus, or having older friends, family members or teachers who have gone there. The trend of recommending the local community college to students, even those who could likely get into more prestigious four-year schools, was a consistent practice. This message not only came from the guidance counselors but some of the teachers as well, some of whom had taken the very same path themselves. In the cases of most River City students, their teachers and guidance counselors were their main source of information on colleges and the college application process. Very few of the students I interviewed had parents who were involved in the college selection or application process.

Teachers and guidance counselors made little acknowledgement of status or quality differences between community college and four-year institutions or even between various four-year colleges and universities. During a conversation with a senior girl which took place in May, she told me that she planned to go to college. I asked her where she had applied, and she informed me that she had not filled out any applications yet. Her lack of knowledge of the timeline of the college application process struck me as I reflected that her options had already been limited by the fact that at this late date she had not yet considered filling out an application. Nevertheless, at the local community college, students were able to simply show up and register a few days before classes without a lengthy application process.

Mike

Mike is a quiet student who takes welding courses at the vocational training center and plays for the school's bowling team. He is a short boy with blonde hair who rarely speaks in class. He has this to say about his future plans.

> **Carrie:** *What do you want to do when you graduate from high school?*

Mike: *I want to do welding [. . .] I'll probably go to a two-year college. Every college has it in the area. VTC offers job opportunities right out of high school.*
Carrie: *What schools have it in the area, do you know?*
Mike: *Valley State does, I know [. . .]*
Carrie: *So, Valley State is something that caught your eye?*
Mike: *Yeah. Actually, that's what my older friends who went to college for welding do. Two of them, so.*
Carrie: *Do you know of any other schools that have welding around here, obviously RCCC does, right?*
Mike: *I think they do, I don't know, I'm not sure.*

Though I interviewed Mike near the end of his junior year and he expressed a desire to go to at least a two-year school, he did not appear to have a great deal of knowledge about colleges or the choices that might be available. His knowledge of programs was gained from older friends and the colleges they chose to attend, like Valley State.

The general lack of knowledge about the college education process that the River City students conveyed stands in stark contrast with upper-middle-class schools, particularly private institutions which often measure their success by the status of the colleges and universities their graduates attend. In many of these schools students are literally taught how to go to college. Not only are the specifics of the application, recommendation, and interview process covered, but the culture of the school encourages students to take classes and participate in activities which will boost their desirability to colleges.[12]

Here, Mike talks about his older siblings who both enrolled in college after high school.

Mike: *My brother goes to State University and my sister goes to RCCC.*
Carrie: *Do they like it?*
Mike: *My brother does but I guess my sister doesn't because she's going to drop out or something.*
Carrie: *How long has she been there?*
Mike: *She went for one year and then she dropped out and then she started going again and she's going to drop out again.*

Despite their comparative lack of knowledge about colleges the River City boys speak comfortably and confidently about the promise of college to fulfill their career plans. The boys who speak about attending college have a variety of future plans. They talk about what degrees and jobs they would like to pursue. Many of them talk about attending River City Community College and the choice of attending RCCC, as most of the students refer to it, is presented by the guidance counselors and many of the teachers as a smart choice. Guidance counselors, like Mr. Ferell, are confident that most River City students can meet the school's standards. In addition, tuition is more affordable than other local private and even state colleges and universities. For those without a strong academic record, attending a community college, they are told by Mr. Ferell, provides them with a chance to boost their grades and save money if they plan to transfer into a four-year school.

Despite all the positive word of mouth that local community college receives from the faculty and administration at River City High School, Mike's story of his sister's struggles there is not an isolated one. Frequently, students told me about siblings or older friends who had enrolled in college after high school and were either struggling now or had dropped out altogether. These common stories beg the question as to how prepared the River City High School students are for college academically, economically, and culturally. This remains an open question which deserves further study.

Many of the River City students approach college as an extension of the high school experience rather than with the more traditional middle-class view of college as a life experience. For example, many of the River City High School students envision themselves living off campus and often keeping their part-time jobs while attending college, as opposed to a more middle- or upper-middle-class version of the college experience including living on campus and participating in multiple aspects of college life.

It could also be argued that after attending community college or even a four-year school, these students might not be in a much better place economically as their own parents were when they graduated from high school with no plans to attend college. The area's struggling economy does not hold great promise for those who plan to stay in the area. As the story of Alicia's mother shows, she feels her secretarial job, which once required only a high school education, is threatened, unless she pursues a college degree—and even then her job is not entirely secure.

Future Plans: Career

When it comes to career choice, the River City boys talk about pursuing jobs such as state trooper, teacher, auto technician, welder, and umpire, to name a few. As noted earlier, many of these jobs are traditionally masculine jobs, such as state trooper, umpire, and welder. Others contain aspects of traditionally feminine work or mental labor, such as teacher and translator. None of the River City boys cited a desire to pursue more traditionally feminine occupations, such as nursing or childcare (though some of the River City fathers were in nursing and related occupations). Some of the jobs the boys talked about contain both feminine and masculine aspects. Social studies teacher is one example of this. Teaching is generally considered a feminine profession and the mental aspect of this job codes it as feminine using a traditional working-class model. However, within the River City High School culture, there are many male social studies teachers who model the role of social studies teacher as a male one.

Brian

Brian, the soccer player, wants to be a physical education teacher. He has this to say:

> **Brian:** *I want to become a gym teacher. I want to do something with sports. Before, I wanted to do, like, physical therapist or something like that. Like, work on something with sports teams. And then, I'm thinking about a p.e. teacher because of all the things my mom says.*
> **Carrie:** *She loves it?*
> **Brian:** *Like the millions of things. Like, my mom just, little kids watching parents and everything like that, watch them hatch. And what the kids say and everything, it's so cute. Little kids and sports or something, I'd like to do something like that.*
> **Carrie:** *So, do you plan to go to college right after high school?*
> **Brian:** *[. . .] I want to stay around here. I was thinking about RCCC maybe. And then going to, like, after RCCC going to a teaching college or something.*
> **Carrie:** *Transferring to a four-year school?*
> **Brian:** *Yeah.*
> **Carrie:** *And would you live at home, do you think, while you're going there?*
> **Brian:** *Yeah. I'm pretty sure.*

Brian, who is estranged from his father, talks about how his mother had positive experiences with teaching and how he would like to teach physical education since it would allow him to combine his love of sports (coded as masculine) with his desire to work with children (coded as feminine).

Aaron

Like Brian, Aaron also wants to be a physical education teacher. Aaron plays both football and baseball for River City High School. Aaron has short, curly, brown hair and often wears t-shirts that advertise beer or liquor. He tells me his teachers would describe him as "lazy," and, in fact, they do. Aaron tells me about his plans after high school.

> **Carrie:** *And what do you plan to do when you graduate from high school?*
> **Aaron:** *Go to college and hopefully become a phys. ed. teacher.*
> **Carrie:** *A phys. ed. teacher? And what made you want to do that?*
> **Aaron:** *Just liking sports all my life.*
> **Carrie:** *Do you think that your education here has prepared you to do what you want to?*
> **Aaron:** *Kinda, just like starting, you know, starting to. I think college will mainly do it.*

> *Carrie: Do you know where you'd like to go to college?*
> *Aaron: Hopefully, like, State University or State College, like,*
> *around here. I don't want to go away. Maybe RCCC or something*
> *if they've got phys. ed. there.*
> *Carrie: Would you live at home or in a dorm?*
> *Aaron: At home. Save my money.*

Teaching physical education is a traditionally masculine occupation and most often includes coaching sports teams, as well. As mentioned, mental labor is equated with femininity and physical labor with masculinity.[13] Willis's comparison of mental and physical labor equates the mental occupations with femininity and physical ones with masculinity. Though the profession of teaching physical education in many cases requires a college degree, and indeed these boys plan to pursue one, the occupation itself is one that stresses the physical and, thereby, the masculine.

Many of the boys who are involved in vocational training discuss continuing their education at Valley State,[*] a regional state college that specializes in vocational education.

Joseph

Joseph and Bob both would like to go to college at Valley State. Joseph, who plays football, reflects on his future plans.

> *Carrie: What do you plan to do when you graduate from high*
> *school?*
> *Joseph: I'm going to be an auto technician or an auto designer.*
> *Carrie: Auto designer—what's an auto designer do?*
> *Joseph: They design new types of cars, engines, all types of stuff.*
> *Carrie: OK. So, all the new stuff?*
> *Joseph: Yeah, yeah.*
> *Carrie: And what kind of education do you need for that?*
> *Joseph: Two-year or four-year school. Certain design CAD or*
> *[inaudible] or technician or something else. I don't remember.*

Joseph's plans span a wide range. While an auto technician's job is more hands-on and technical and does not necessarily require a great deal of education, an auto designer would likely require a different type of education, engineering courses and possibly graduate work. Like Casey from the girls' section, who considers becoming either an Emergency Medical Technician or a pediatrician, Joseph's consideration of future careers lacks knowledge of the required levels of education. While this lack of knowledge may not work to prevent these students from pursuing either career, it is a unique marker of a class-based understanding of higher education.

---

[*] Valley State is a pseudonym.

Bob

Bob also reflects on his current situation and what his future might look like.

> *Bob: Yeah, I work at Super-Market. That's a fun job, let me tell*
> *you.*
> *Carrie: Are you being facetious?*
> *Bob: No, I'm kidding. It sucks. I liked it, at first, but then it's just*
> *like 'Aawww'—I feel like a machine. It's so repetitive. You do the*
> *same thing over again on cashier [. . .] I was going to try a job at*
> *the Casino. But I'm going to college in August.*
> *Carrie: Oh you are, where are you going?*
> *Bob: Valley State.*

Bob's current job at Super-Market is not one he wants to continue as full-time work after high school. Unlike some of the VTC students who see themselves continuing their part-time employment after high school Bob is does not view Super-Market as having career potential.

> *Carrie: Where do you picture yourself in five years?*
> *Bob: Just kind of, like, playing it day by day right now. Hopefully,*
> *I'll have, [pause] I hope to have at least, not a house, yet, but*
> *maybe a really nice apartment and a car. Just have all that stuff. I*
> *don't know where, though. Maybe here but I doubt it. There's not*
> *really too much to do around here.*
> *Carrie: Where would you go if you didn't stay here, any ideas?*
> *Bob: I don't know. If me and my girlfriend stay together we'll*
> *probably be in California or Michigan or something like that.*
> *[. . .] Carrie: What about ten years from now?*
> *Bob: Ten years. Hopefully have my own business and a house and*
> *maybe one or two kids.*

Both Joseph and Bob talk about being auto body technicians and going to Valley State. Each are taking auto body classes at the VTC now and plan to continue their education in college where they can also specialize in their chosen field. Here is what the Valley State website says, "Valley State College, a member of the technology college sector [. . .] offers outstanding educational opportunities for students in its nearly sixty associate degree programs, twelve baccalaureate degree programs, and several certificate programs. Numerous vocational-technical offerings stressing hands-on learning are available at the School of Applied Technology Campus..."[14]

Lloyd

Lloyd talks about his two ideas: either to attend River City Community College right after high school or get certified as an umpire.

> *Carrie:* So, what are your plans when you graduate from high
> school?
> *Lloyd:* I would like to go to college. What I'm planning on doing
> with security, I'm planning on going to RCCC for two years and
> transfer to either State College or Waterville and finish up. Be-
> cause I want to be a state trooper, if I'm [doing something] police-
> related. But if I go the other way and decide I want to be a base-
> ball umpire, then after high school, I turn eighteen, I'd probably
> go to one of those schools and then get the instruction and training
> and everything and then apply for a job, that way [. . .]
> *Carrie:* Would you live at home while you were doing that?
> *Lloyd:* Probably. It's not that far away. I wouldn't see the reason
> to stay on campus there.
> *Carrie:* What about having a job, do you think you would work
> while doing that?
> *Lloyd:* Yeah, I'd definitely have to, to try to pay for it. I mean I
> have money in the bank but it wouldn't cover it all I don't think. I
> have to see, you know. RCCC isn't that expensive, but the others
> are.

Lloyd expresses his concern about paying for college. He tells me "RCCC isn't that expensive, but the others are." Lloyd's father is disabled and his mother works two jobs to help support the family, so money to pay for college or umpire school is a very real consideration for Lloyd.

Again, Lloyd, like many of the River City students, does not consider taking loans to pay for college. He couches his discussion in terms of paying for college entirely with money he has earned.

Doug

Doug, who plays hockey for the school, plans to attend college after high school. Last year, he wanted to be an attorney, but this year he decided he would rather be a high school teacher because he feels it would be less stressful and more fun. Both of Doug's parents dropped out of high school and earned their GEDs. Here, he speaks about his parents and his plans after high school.

> *Carrie:* Did either of them [your parents] go to college?
> *Doug:* Nope. They're pretty psyched about that, too. They'd bet-
> ter be paying for that, too. They said they were but I'd better hold
> them to it. I plan on moving out next month.
> *Carrie:* Oh really?
> *Doug:* Yeah, me and my friend George are going to get an apart-
> ment together. So, they better pay for my college.
> *Carrie:* Where do you want to go to school?

> *Doug:* *The first two years I'm going to go to RCCC, and then I'm going to go to State College for the other [two years].*

Doug tells me that his parents told him they would pay for college, and yet he notes, "They said they were but I'd better hold them to it," as if he doubts that they will actually follow through. Doug's parents are divorced—his mother is a manager of a local convenience store and his father does maintenance work for River City. Unlike a few of the students whose parents are involved in the college selection process, Doug seems to be on his own. His parents, having never attended college, are likely unfamiliar with how admissions work. Later, Doug tells me that his other option was to go to a regional public college but he decided against that.

> *Carrie:* *So, have you told your parents about the apartment yet?*
> *Doug:* *Yep, oh, my mom was all for it. Her other option was me going away to college, and she didn't want that.*
> *Carrie:* *Did you want to?*
> *Doug:* *Well, I was thinking about going to Rockside. But, you know, I can't just move out [of town]. Besides, I don't want to leave home. I have too many strings.*

Like many of the River City teens I spoke with, either the teens themselves or their parents (or both) were reluctant about their leaving town for college. This sentiment was expressed by both the boys and the girls. For Doug, this idea is articulated by telling me, "I have too many strings." Other students, like Benjamin, directly connect staying in River City to economic necessity. Still others, like Rachel and Alex, talk about their parents' preferences that they stay nearby. Within this school and community simply "going to college" seems synonymous with an accepted level of success. There is little acknowledgment by students, teachers and even the guidance counselors of the college hierarchy. Just as getting the right answer is stressed in classes, obtaining the college credential is stressed over the social and cultural learning experience of attending college.

Military Considerations

Many of the boys, including some considering college after high school, discuss the possibility of being involved in military service. In contrast, only one girl, Casey, talked about the military as a possibility for her future. As mentioned earlier, guidance counselor Mr. Ferell presents the students' options after high school in three main categories; work, college, and military. In addition, the military has a visible presence at River City High School. A uniformed recruiter visits often and talks to students in a room called the career center.

During my fieldwork, I encountered a handful of students who talked about planning to enroll in the military. The career center, located on the first floor of the school, was a space where students could do research on colleges and careers and also played host to military recruiters who had a visible presence at the school, where they recruited in uniform.

Ross

Ross is on the football team and hopes to play in college by earning a scholarship. He tells me that his first choice of colleges is a military academy.

> *Carrie: Are you trying to get a football scholarship or anything like that?*
> *Ross: Yeah, I'm trying to go to college to play football and hopefully get some scholarships. Probably not athletic because they'd be division three, and they don't have athletic scholarships but I can probably get something academic having to do with football.*
> *Carrie: What kind of schools are you looking at?*
> *Ross: Actually, some private and some public like Brookville College and Appleton State College. [Colleges] most people look at from our school in the past couple years. And I get letters from a bunch of schools, and some of them I just kind of throw away a little bit and then some of them I read. Kings Point is a school I want to go to but I don't think I'm going to get in.*
> *Carrie: What's Kings Point, a private school?*
> *Ross: United States Merchant Marine Academy. It's pretty hard to get in.*

Ross talks about the multiple options which he is considering as a result of his talent playing football and his academic accomplishments. Prowess on the sports field is highly admired at River City High School, and Mr. Ferell, the guidance counselor, is quick to mention to his students that many of River City's alumni continue playing sports in college. As part of his introduction to the college application process for juniors, he includes a reminder that all students who plan to play a sport in college must complete a NCAA form, which he has available.

Dirk

Dirk is a tall, thin boy with short, brown hair who often wears a baseball cap backwards and a leather necklace. He speaks about going into the military as one of his options after high school, and he is one of the few students who acknowledge the war when talking about his future plans to go into the military.

> *Carrie: What do you want to do after high school?*
> *Dirk: Well, I want to do the Marine reserves thing. I wanted to go into active but then I realized there's a war, so I'd better stay out. I thought the reserves would be a good idea for the money. After*

that, I wanted to try to get an apprenticeship as either a mason or a carpenter. Overall, in life, I want to try to open my own business.

Nevertheless, Dirk's distinction between the reserves and active duty proves to be false reasoning as the war in Iraq has resulted in many reservists being called to active service.

Lloyd

Lloyd, who wants either to be a state trooper or a baseball umpire, talks about considering the military.

> *Carrie: How do you think your ideas of what you want to do after high school compare with your friends? Do they have similar ideas or different things?*
> *Lloyd: Different, definitely different. Well, there's kids in my class, there's, like, two of them that go to River City that are in my field, that are in the field that I want to do, police work. But it's all different than what I want to do. I want to be a state trooper, and my friend, Larry, he wants to have to do with military police. Working on an air force base or something like that. I mean, I don't really know too many people who are going to be a police officer.*
> *Carrie: Are a lot of your friends planning on going to college or not?*
> *Lloyd: Yeah. Well, they're going to use the military to get through college, to pay for it, you know. Which isn't a bad idea. I'm thinking about doing it myself.*
> *Carrie: Have you looked into that at all?*
> *Lloyd: My friend's dad, he's a staff sergeant of the Air Force, so I talked to him about it.*
> *Carrie: Are you leaning toward that or is that just another option right now?*
> *Lloyd: It's an option. I'm thinking about it, you know. I'm looking at the advantages and disadvantages of it. I'm not really sure if I want to do it right yet.*
> *Carrie: What are the advantages and disadvantages as far as you know?*
> *Lloyd: Advantages are you get paid to do it and they pay for your college. It's good to serve your country. You feel proud, you know, if you do get called to duty. Disadvantages are when you sign up, you're signed in there for, like, four years. There's no backing out of it once you're signed up. That's pretty much the only disadvantage of it. And also, when you sign, it's eight years—like, four years you serve and after that, the four years when you're done,*

you're still on the list for four years. If they need you for a war,
they can call you and use you.

As mentioned earlier, guidance counselor Mr. Ferell discusses the students' options after school in three main categories; work, college, or military. Despite the fact that those joining the military would likely be sent to Iraq, this was never mentioned by Mr. Ferell when he spoke about the pros and cons of joining the military. It was as if he kept the same speech he had used for years despite the changing political climate. I did, however, observe one teacher address the question of fighting in Iraq with a senior who had already enrolled in the military.

Joining the military, arguably, may be one of the few traditionally male working-class occupations left for the boys of River City. Military service only requires a high school diploma, stresses manual labor over mental and is certainly coded as masculine. In addition, though a military career may or may not pay enough to support a family on a single salary, for a man, the job encourages at least the centrality of his career, as frequent relocation is the norm and the ability to leave home for long periods of time is a necessity.

Looking into the Future

While many of the boys talked about staying in the area directly after high school, when I asked the question, "Where do you see yourself five years from now?" some of them discussed moving to different parts of the country. Many spoke about staying in the area, yet places like the South were mentioned more than once as a place that not only offered a mild climate, but where they thought it would be easier to find a good job.

Joseph

Some of the boys, like Joseph, refer to either traveling to these places already or having a relative who lives there.

> *Carrie: Would you like to stay in New York?*
> *Joseph: No, definitely got to get out of New York.*
> *Carrie: Where would you go?*
> *Joseph: Florida. South somewhere.*
> *Carrie: Is that a weather thing?*
> *Joseph: Yeah, definitely the weather thing*

Lloyd

Lloyd thinks about moving to Georgia, where his older brother lives. He explains:

Lloyd: *Five years from now, if I plan on going with the police job or whatever, if I'm going to go to college for that, I see myself in academy training. Either in academy training or in college. Ending college. Going toward it because you need a four-year degree. So, it would probably be college that I'd be in. I'd be around twenty-two so I'd probably still be in college.*

Carrie: *You'd probably just be graduating.*

Lloyd: *Yeah. But if I go with the umpire thing, I might be a lower-class umpire, like maybe class A or a rookie league. Working my way up. They say it takes eight to twelve years to get to AAA where the Grizzlys are. The next step up is the pros.*

Carrie: *What about ten years from now?*

Lloyd: *Ten years, ten years with the police, I'd probably be being on the State troopers, being a member of the State trooper's squad.*

Carrie: *Would you picture yourself still here in New York or in River City?*

Lloyd: *No, I'd probably be in Georgia if I decided to do that.*

Carrie: *Why would you go there? Because your brother is there?*

Lloyd: *That and because I've visited so many times. I just love it down there. The weather's nice and they pay a hell of a lot more. They pay a lot more than up here than they would. There's a lot more people down there, too, and they drive crazy on the highway. They need some state police down there because it's crazy.*

Carrie: *What about where you would live—a house, an apartment?*

Lloyd: *To start out, I'd probably go with an apartment until I got my bank account worked up to where I could afford a house and be able to put payments and all that kind of thing. Like a down payment and then payments on a house, like that.*

Carrie: *Do you picture yourself with a family some day?*

Lloyd: *It depends. If I go with the umpire thing, I'm going to be traveling nine months out of the year, so I don't think it would be a wise decision to be doing that. But if I go with the police career, I'd love to, I mean, I get along well with kids, I'd love to have some of my own someday.*

Lloyd has a fairly well constructed sense his future. In fact, he takes into account the possible difficulties of being both an umpire and a family man. While this critique of the job does not take on the economic tone that Maria's or Chloe's who found that dancing and skating were not economically practical for them to pursue, it is similar to Amanda's critique of working with a traveling theater company.

Dirk

Dirk also considered the military but told me, "I wanted to go into active but then I realized there's a war, so I'd better stay out." Dirk, whose father is a network representative at an automobile factory and whose mother is a secretary, plans to do masonry work when he is done with high school. He talks about his future plans to move out of River City and his love of traveling.

> *Carrie: Where do you picture yourself five years from now?*
> *Dirk: [laughs] My mom keeps saying jail but I don't think I'm going to go that far.*
> *Carrie: Why does she say jail?*
> *Dirk: Well, when I first got my license, I got into a car accident which was my fault. Two cars, yeah, a three-car accident. And you know how I said I didn't have insurance on my car? Well, I needed to get somewhere the one day, so I took my car out. And I put fake plates on it. So I got written up for five tickets.*
> *[. . .] Carrie: So, if you're not in jail, what would you do then?*
> *Dirk: I don't know actually. I live by day to day. I love to travel so who knows?*
> *Carrie: Where would you like to travel to, what are some of the places you want to go?*
> *Dirk: I don't know. I've always wanted to go to New Orleans for Mardi Gras. And the Bahamas for Junkano, which is pretty much like a Mardi Gras in the Caribbean. [. . .]*
> *Carrie: What do you think about ten years from now, any kind of ideas of what you'd like to accomplish by that point?*
> *Dirk: I'm hoping that I'll probably have my own business or be starting on my way to have my own business. That would be nice.*
> *Carrie: What about a family, have you thought about having your own family at all?*
> *Dirk: The more I look at my parents, it doesn't look like you want to jump into that sort of thing. You want to take your time and find the right person and that sort of thing.*
> *Carrie: That's smart.*
> *Dirk: Yeah.*

A handful of the boys I interviewed discussed moving out of River City at some time in the future. Some of the reasons that the boys cited for this were; liking to travel, as Joseph and Dirk talk about, and seeking out a more prosperous city, as Lloyd mentions. In contrast, the reasons girls cited for possibly leaving River City in the future were specifically career-oriented, for example, Chloe and Nicole were interested in fashion design and saw themselves moving to New York City, while Jaime said she felt moving out of River City was a sign of success.

Most of the girls and boys who spoke with me planned to go to college after high school. For most River City students college offers them an opportunity to be more educated than many of their parents. Though both girls and boys want to go to college the motivations for doing so are different. Girls talk about financial security and being able to provide for themselves and possibly future families as an important motivation for going to college. Boys, on the other hand, talked about choosing to go to college because of the specific career they wanted to pursue. Each of these articulations reveals assumptions about the gendered roles the girls and boys expect to fill in the future. Both the girls and the boys work with traditional gender roles, as well as new articulations of gender in order to form their conceptions of their future gendered selves.

Most of the boys gravitate toward traditionally male occupations and often ones that also rely on physical, rather than mental, labor. This trend was stressed in Willis's study of working class lads. Even the four boys who want to be teachers chose traditionally male subjects: physical education (two boys) and history (two boys). Not one of the boys chose high status jobs such as doctors or lawyers, though one wanted to pursue sports medicine. In addition, only four boys cited occupations which centered on mental labor: history teachers (two boys), translator and sports management (which includes mental labor but also management of athletes). Significantly different from previous documented generations of working-class young men is that the great majority wanted to attend college. In fact, all but one to them who spoke with me expressed a desire to attend college. This generation is beginning to look outside of their community, though arguably for most not very far, for opportunity and a new self-definition tied to education and credentials.

Also unlike previous generations of working-class young men, they do not relate their social position to that of women as a way to claim relative privilege, superiority, or power. This kind of comparison would not hold up, as the girls are pursing ostensibly the same futures as the boys in the educational and economic spheres. In light of this the boys seem to be turning toward a perceived opportunity (in this case mainly educational) as a way of defining themselves. Unfortunately, it seems certain they will encounter many barriers in their pursuit of this opportunity, possibly academic and certainly economic. Work by Bloom documents the many economic hurdles low-income and working-class students must overcome, and often do not, in order to stay in school.[15]

White working-class girls express a strong identification with their mothers and find purpose within this, unlike the boys who do not seem to have found a meaningful or comfortable way to identify themselves within their community after high school. While the girls express solidarity with their mothers, the boys do not seem to engage with their family struggles in the same ways. The girls, to some extent, acknowledge the gendered aspects of the familial, educational, and economic struggles they have witnessed and of which they have sometimes been a part. Only a small group of the boys interviewed acknowledged their families' struggles, and when they did, their approaches were more likely to take on a protective tone.

As the girls sought to pursue college education mainly from necessity often derived from family struggles, the boys sought a college education but did not articulate it as a necessity, economic or otherwise, in most cases. The boys instead viewed college as an opportunity of which they were personally poised to take advantage. Therefore, the pressures boys felt to attend college came from the outside, parental or teacher expectations, rather than an internalized sense of necessity brought to light by adversity, as in the case of the girls.

Just as the girls in Weis's *Working Class Without Work* experienced moments of critique, the River City girls experience certain moments, too.[16] Their critiques were built around feelings of solidarity with their mothers. This gender consciousness borders on class consciousness as the girls try to understand the struggles they are bracing themselves for in the future, the same struggles many have seen their mothers endure. One explanation for this might be that often in cases of divorce, women face more economic difficulties than men. Sometimes postponing their own education to raise families, often being the primary custodial parent, and facing economic hardships, it is disproportionately the women who, in turn, relate and share these struggles more intimately with their daughters who may one day face them themselves. The River City girls who critique their families' struggles are now developing ideas about their futures and the roles they want to play, many of them striving to avoid the struggles they have witnessed and experienced.

Framed by their class position, financial necessity is primary for the girls. In comparison with the girls' attention to these issues, the boys' silence around them, which seems like denial in some cases, is even more striking. The boys are not in tune with the struggles of their families and in the few cases when these are acknowledged, there is no further attempt to relate their own families' situations with that of other mothers, fathers, or families in their class. It appears as though a construction of masculinity, including a male in the role of worker and provider, does not allow the acknowledgement of a class-wide absence of this role and the boys desire to fill that role themselves in some way. Even the boys who witness their single mothers supporting their families bemoan the absence of a male provider and attempt to fill the role themselves as protectors.

Though financial necessity was central in the girls' conceptions of their future roles, it appears less prominent among the boys' concerns. The boys expressed more confidence that they would be able to marry, buy a house, and live where they wanted to when they were older without facing setbacks or struggles. As in previous studies, the girls at River City were thinking ahead about providing adequately for themselves, something that impacted their career choices.[17] River City boys, unlike in previous studies of working-class boys, were focused on college.[18] However, they did not speak critically about questioning whether or not they would actually be able to provide for themselves and their families after college.

The masculine role which the boys are negotiating, particularly as it relates to economics, is a complicated and somewhat contradictory one. The traditional working-class male role of provider is generally one the boys cling to (though the type of job they will have has often changed from the traditional models). They express confidence that they will find decent jobs and eventually own a house and have a job they will have has often changed from the traditional models). They express confidence that they will find decent jobs and eventually own a house and have a family. Despite this, the boys do accept the logic of a two-income household as the norm. Possibly the largest contrast here comes from the ways the girls focus on careers as primary and marriage as coming later while the boys focus on their career as primary and many envision marriage and/or families happening simultaneously with the development of their career.

Unlike the girls who have accepted that their futures will likely include struggles, the boys are able to position themselves as part of an average group whose opportunities will be no more or less than any other group. The themes of normality and lack of solidarity, class-based or otherwise, is one I will explore over the next two chapters. In chapter five, I begin by discussing peer groups and some of the ways group identity is acknowledged at River City High School. In chapter six, I develop this discussion into one of larger group's perceptions of normality and race, which have contributed to both the girls' and boys' perceptions expressed in chapters three and four particularly as they relate to issues of group identity and the possibility of openings for gender, class, and racial critiques of society and its economic structure in particular.

Notes

1. Willis, P. *Learning to Labor: How Working Class Kids Get Working Class Jobs*. New York: Columbia University Press, 1977.

2. Weis, L. *Class Reunion: The Remaking of the American White Working Class*. New York: Routledge, 2004; Weis, L. *Working Class without Work: High School Students in a Deindustrializing Economy*. New York: Routledge, 1990.

3. Willis, P. *Learning to Labor: How Working Class Kids Get Working Class Jobs*. New York: Columbia University Press, 1977; Weis, L. *Working Class without Work: High School Students in a Deindustrializing Economy*. New York: Routledge, 1990.

4. Willis, P. *Learning to Labor: How Working Class Kids Get Working Class Jobs*. New York: Columbia University Press, 1977.

5. Mac an Ghaill, M. *The Making of Men: Masculinities, Sexualities and Schooling*. Buckingham: Open University Press, 1994; Imms, W. "Multiple Masculinities and the Schooling of Boys." *Canadian Journal of Education* 25, no. 2 (2000): 152–65.

6. Imms, W. "Multiple Masculinities and the Schooling of Boys." *Canadian Journal of Education* 25, no. 2 (2000): 152–65.

7. Reich, R. *I'll Be Short: Essentials for a Decent Working Society*. Boston: Beacon Press, 2002; Weis, L. *Working Class without Work: High School Students in a Deindustrializing Economy*. New York: Routledge, 1990; Willis, P. *Learning to Labor: How Working Class Kids Get Working Class Jobs*. New York: Columbia University Press, 1977.

8. Ehrenreich, B. *Nickel and Dimed: On (Not) Getting by in America*. New York: Metropolitan Books, 2001; Willis, P. *Learning to Labor: How Working Class Kids Get Working Class Jobs*. New York: Columbia University Press, 1977.

9. Willis, P. *Learning to Labor: How Working Class Kids Get Working Class Jobs*. New York: Columbia University Press, 1977. 126.

11. Willis, P. *Learning to Labor: How Working Class Kids Get Working Class Jobs.* New York: Columbia University Press, 1977. 104.

12. St. George, K. "Rethinking Reproduction: The Role of One Private, Catholic, and All-Girl High School in the Identity Development of the Young Women Who Attend." dissertation, University at Buffalo, The State University of New York, 2004.

13. Willis, P. *Learning to Labor: How Working Class Kids Get Working Class Jobs.* New York: Columbia University Press, 1977; Weis, L. *Working Class without Work: High School Students in a Deindustrializing Economy.* New York: Routledge, 1990.

14. Valley State Website. 2003. Valley State is a pseudonym.

15. Bloom, J. "Hollowing the Promise of Higher Education: Inside the Political Economy of Access to College." In *Beyond Silenced Voices: Class, Race and Gender in United States Schools,* edited by L. Weis and M. Fine. Albany: SUNY Press, 2005.

16. Weis, L. *Working Class without Work: High School Students in a Deindustrializing Economy.* New York: Routledge, 1990.

17. Weiler, J.D. *Codes and Contradictions: Race, Gender Identity, and Schooling.* Albany: SUNY Press, 2000; Weis, L. *Working Class without Work: High School Students in a Deindustrializing Economy.* New York: Routledge, 1990.

18. Willis, P. *Learning to Labor: How Working Class Kids Get Working Class Jobs.* New York: Columbia University Press, 1977.

Chapter Four

Peer Groups

It's all about the cheerleaders and the jocks. You're nobody unless you're a rah-rah.
Megan —age eighteen

Peer groups are a central form of identification at River City High and students identified others and often themselves by their peer group association. At River City High School peer groups were most obviously identified by a student's appearance; including clothing and hairstyle, but also by the behavior of students in each group and what activities, particularly school-sanctioned activities, in which they participated. Groups include the preps, jocks, cheerleaders, smart kids, hippies, and punks (also called the freaks). While students were easily able to name and identify groups that existed at their school, they were often reluctant to identify themselves as a member of one group. This reluctance to self-label is something explored later in this chapter.

The students at River City High are not a racially, economically or religiously diverse group. According to the 2000 Census, 97.9 percent of the city residents are white and this is reflected in the student body.[1] At the high school level, 98.5 percent of the students identify as white, 1.0 percent as American Indian, Alaskan, Asian or Pacific Islander, 0.2 percent black, and 0.5 percent Hispanic.[2] Though there is a small group of students whose families have recently emigrated from Eastern Europe, these students are only visible as "others" when they speak to each other in their families' language. The year I was at River City High I observed only one class with a student of color, a Latino, whose family was originally from Puerto Rico and now established in River City. In addition, I met only one Muslim student, who told me she was one of two Muslim students in the entire school. I did not observe any classes with African-American students and saw only one African-American teacher during my fieldwork. One way the students in this largely homogenous group differentiate themselves is by identifying with peer groups. When the white students who I interviewed spoke of diversity within their school, they pointed to the existence of different peer groups as an example of this diversity.

In *Shades of White*, Perry discusses clique membership. She states:

> the overarching organizing principle behind clique membership was a norm-other semiotic code, with 'norm' being those who more or less enforced the mainstream expectations of the school and wider society (the popular and normal kids) and 'other' being those who stood outside those

73

popular and normal kids) and 'other' being those who stood outside those parameters in one way or another (the smoker/skaters, hicks, and homies).[3]

It is clear from the literature that boys and girls have different experiences in school. Students of different ethnic, racial or class backgrounds also have profoundly different school experiences (though students of similar classes, genders, or racial/ethnic groups do not necessarily share the same experiences). Peer groups and other forms of social organization that happen within high schools play important roles for students. What students learn, how they learn it, the type of cultural capital they are exposed to, and their perceptions of future roles are all reflected in the social groups they are a part of in high school. Those who study these groups have made significant connections between the high school experience and adult social and economic roles.

Eckert's study, *Jocks and Burnouts,* focuses on dual in-school cultures, based on class differences that are formed and maintained in the school setting. Her discussion frames the groups she calls jocks and burnouts as separate cliques that are divided along class lines. Eckert then explains how the cliques work to perpetuate a hierarchy within the school and how this hierarchy establishes patterns for the reproduction of class. The jocks, who are defined as middle class, identify with school authority, participate in school-based extra-curricular activities and win the approval of their teachers. The burnouts, more often the working-class students, resist school authority, generally do not participate in school-based extra-curricular activities, and resist the rules and structure of the school.[4]

Brantlinger's study of social class and politics in secondary schools also focuses on the role of cliques, specifically as mechanisms of social reproduction. This analysis clarifies the ways in which cliques operate as hierarchies but also explains that these social constructions are in a constant state of flux and negotiation. Brantlinger's examination highlights the roles of both structure and agency as part of secondary school culture.[5]

Epstein and Karweit also look at the operation of social systems in secondary schools. Extracurricular activities, official and hidden curriculum, and peer interactions are all important aspects of social organization which, the authors note, has long-standing consequences for students for which this type of social selection, "is no isolated event but rather has lasting consequences for the social relationships it spawns."[6]

Peer Groups and Identity

Like the students Perry, Eckert, Brantlinger, and Epstein & Karweit studied, the students at River City also divided themselves into cliques.[7] When asked to describe what groups existed at their school, the students of River City named various cliques (e.g., jocks, hippies, etc.). Teachers also acknowledged cliques within the school, though they often hesitated to use the students' names for the groups, particularly those that were derogatory, such as "freaks" or "druggies." Within this racially homogeneous environment, cliques are a significant hierarchical form of social organization. In racially diverse settings students usually divide themselves into groups based on their racial and ethnic identities.[8] White students in racially homogenous settings tend to see race as a neutral category and as socially and politically insignificant. In addition, these white students refer to non-racial categories in order to socially and politically organize themselves.[9] At River City, most students were white and from a similar class background and the students talked about diversity and difference in terms of the cliques to which they belonged.

Identification with or distance from school-sanctioned activities and school culture, in general, is a strong determining factor for peer group membership and group identity within the school setting. Rachel, a soft-spoken girl who played on the school's girls' softball and soccer teams, consistently had some of the highest test scores in her social studies class and had this to say when I asked her "What do you like about your school?"

> **Rachel:** *There's a lot of different people so some of my friends are different from other friends, and they wouldn't be friends themselves but I can still hang out with them. The diversity of different kinds of people.*
> **Carrie:** *Like what kinds of people?*
> **Rachel:** *Some people are this kind or some people are like that. Like, some of my friends aren't really athletic but I have friends who are from my soccer team or softball team.*

Students also divide along the more subtle lines of social class and economic distinctions.[10] Brantlinger explores some of the ways students separate themselves and are separated into cliques in the school environment according to the social class of their parents.[11] Students from "settled living" families, often with more stable economic situations often fall into the categories of "preppie," "smart," "rich," or "popular," and "hard living" or lower income students fall into more negative categories such as "druggie," "smoker," or "stupid." This phenomenon is not solely driven by students or teachers, but is also embedded in the hidden curriculum which often steers privileged students toward more prestigious courses and less privileged students toward remedial or lower level coursework as well as vocational training.

Eckert limits her focus to two prominent cliques within the high school setting she studied: the "jocks" and the "burnouts." The jocks were the students that came from middle-class backgrounds while the burnouts were identified as working class. Though there were other cliques at the school, her focus on these two groups highlights the role of school authority in the formation of the identities of both of these groups. She explains:

> The Jock category, based on participation in school activities and closely articulated with the adult power structure of the school, develops a corporate orientation that yields hierarchical social networks and instills corpo-

rate values in personal relations. The Burnout category, focusing on the more immediate development of adult status as defined in the working class world, develops egalitarian social networks focused on transcending the school context. [12]

However, the clear-cut distinction Eckert offers in which "jocks" are middle-class students and "burnouts" are working class was not something I found at River City. The peer groups at River City High School are not so predictably based on social class distinctions as one might expect to find in a more diverse community. Though economic differences exist between families in the River City community, the social class differences are less pronounced. When factors such as parents' education, job, and cultural capital of families are taken into account, the River City community emerges as one largely made up of working-class families. The economic distinctions that do exist among students are often marked by their cars, clothing, and ability to participate in certain extra-curricular activities (i.e. those who do not need to work for all of their spending money have more time to participate in extra-curricular activities and those who are more able to afford equipment or fees for those activities). While a family's economic status impacts a student's ability to purchase the semiotic markers which note peer group affiliation, such as brand name clothing, the majority of students I interviewed had part-time jobs and paid for their clothes, car insurance, gas, and entertainment themselves. Only one student I interviewed, Dana, talked about contributing some of her own income to her family thereby leaving her less spending money of her own.

The social hierarchy of River City does not correspond directly with past studies of peer groups and social class,[13] and the peer groups do not neatly divide along predictable lines as obvious class distinctions were not readily identifiable among the River City students. Therefore to better understand the nature of socio-economic differences that do exist within this working-class population I turn to Weis's exploration of the new white working class in which she makes a distinction between "settled living" and "hard living" working-class lifestyles. "Settled living" refers to a way of life in which working-class families are able to transgress traditional occupational and gender boundaries in order to live in an economically stable environment. The new settled working-class lifestyle is:

> dependent upon having a partner with whom one can merge money—a partner with whom one also shares the day-to-day, minute-by-minute work of parenting following the birth of children. Without this work around the domestic sphere, the 'settled' life with its potentially accompanying and valued (partially class-coded) material and social goods—including homes, NASCAR tickets (auto racing), fireplaces, barbecue pits, wet bars, dirt bikes, cabins for hunting, professional football and hockey tickets, and so forth—simply could not be accomplished.[14]

In contrast, "hard living" describes a working-class lifestyle that clings to a traditional hegemonic working-class masculinity and therefore forgoes the economic and social benefits of a settled lifestyle. Without a willingness to move away from traditional gendered boundaries, at least in action if not verbally, working-class men and women find that it is extremely difficult, if not impossible, to follow a traditional working-class model in which a man financially supports a family doing manual labor and a woman stays home and attends to domestic work. Those "hard livers" who do not explore new options find themselves in a constant state of economic struggle and uncertainty.

Using the patterns of "settled living" and "hard living" (and acknowledging that these categories present a trajectory of ways of living and thinking and that one individual might move between or within them) allows me to identify different levels of privilege and possibility within the working-class community of River City. The "hard living" and "settled living" distinctions help to explain why there are economic and lifestyle divisions among a group where educational achievement, occupational status, and cultural capital are relatively similar.

To highlight the elasticity of these categories I turn to accounts from River City students and their families. For example, some of the River City students move between the categories as a result of divorce and changes in family structure or domestic arrangements. Amanda and Dan both experienced divorce in their families recently and, as a result, are facing economic uncertainty. They discuss the ways their lives are changing as a result of the loss of their "settled" households. Amanda reflects on the loss of material goods, such as the jet-ski her step-father owns. She also notes that before the divorce she expected her family would pay for college, yet now she realizes that her mother will not be able to afford it and she will likely have to pay for college by herself. This realization tempts her to postpone college in favor of a full-time job and therefore has a very real and immediate impact on her future plans.

Dan reflects less on the material losses but expresses a desire to step in and play the role of a "settled" male by caring for his mother's new baby when she works the night shift. Though his mother has a boyfriend who moved in with them, the man is a "hard liver." Dan notes that he comes and goes and cannot be relied upon to provide for them financially or domestically, by helping to care for the baby. Dan finds himself striving for a settled lifestyle in the face of economic and domestic forces pushing his family toward hard living. By volunteering to step into a non-traditional role of care giver for an infant Dan is reinterpreting his own (masculine) role in order to establish a settled lifestyle.

Gwen reflects on how she and her family have moved from a hard living lifestyle, after her father abandoned the family, to the settled living life she lives now. As a single parent, Gwen's mother worked multiple jobs to provide for her children for many years. After her mother remarried, Gwen was able to experience a settled lifestyle of comparable luxury. For these students, economic stability is closely tied to their parents' marital and domestic situations as well as their employment status. These statuses are subject to change over time and many of the River City teens have experienced both hard living times as well as settled living times over the course of their young lives.

These examples illustrate how easy it is for working-class families to move from an economically stable existence to an unstable one. Importantly, Weis's categories of settled and hard living are closely tied to the ways gender roles are acted out. The River City students illustrate how even those who aspire to settled living lifestyles sometimes fail to achieve them due to a variety of circumstances including divorce, death of a spouse, and disability or job loss. These families do not necessarily embrace the ideology of hard livers or necessarily ascribe to a hegemonic working-class masculinity yet they may find themselves in materially similar circumstances to the hard livers. The very stability that the settled living category depends upon is frustratingly illusive for some of these families who ideologically strive for this lifestyle.

Interactions with school-sponsored activities are a primary way students in a largely homogeneous community identify themselves in relation and opposition to their peers. At River City, much like at Eckert's Belten High School, groups of students form their identities within and in opposition to the school culture, which is often highlighted by participation in curricular and extra-curricular activities.[15] This chapter addresses the most visible form of student differentiation at the school, peer group membership, and the ways identification or non-identification with the school culture informs group identities.

The peer group to which a student belongs correlates, to a great extent, with the settled and hard living categories. A student's ability to participate in extra-curricular activities, socializing outside of school, and school events like fieldtrips is sharply influenced by his or her economic and domestic situation (for example, how many hours he or she works at job and how much he or she is required to be at home for tasks such as taking care of younger siblings). Dan and Maria are both examples of students who are in the process of dropping out of high-status extra-curricular activities (football and cheerleading) at the same time as their families are going through major changes (in Dan's case the birth of a baby and in Maria's case a divorce).

Jocks, Cheerleaders, Hippies, Freaks, and Smart Kids

Athletics are important to the culture of River City High School. Within the school community, students, teachers, and administrators support sports and athletes and encourage school spirit surrounding supporting sports teams and specifically the boys' football, basketball, and baseball teams. Football is the most popular sport and gets a great deal of attention from both the school and the community. The team was undefeated during the year I worked in the school. Students and teachers are encouraged in the daily morning announcements to attend sporting events. Those students who participate are sometimes afforded both formal and informal privileges by the faculty and staff.

Cheerleading is also extremely popular and visible within the school. On game days, cheerleaders dress in all or part of their uniforms. Girls on sports teams, such as lacrosse and softball, did the same on their game days. Jaime, who is described next, is both a cheerleader and softball player who participates in the school ritual of wearing her uniforms on game days.

Jaime is an eleventh grader. She is a cheerleader who also participates in softball, band, and numerous extra-curricular clubs. She describes herself as "outgoing" and puts daily effort into her appearance. Her shoulder-length blonde hair is styled every day, frequently in a different way, and her outfits are coordinated—often with matching shoes and purses. Jaime wears her cheerleading or softball uniforms to school on game days. The cheerleading uniform consists of a fitted top with the school letters sewn to the front (during the colder months the girls often wear turtlenecks underneath these tops) and traditional cheerleading skirts in coordinating school colors. The softball uniform consists of a jersey and matching shorts. On game days, even the ribbons in Jaime's hair coordinate with the school colors, and occasionally she wears the spirited ribbons on non-game days, too. Her intense school spirit is marked by her physical appearance and her participation. On a field trip she led the bus of students and chaperones in a "spirit cheer," one of the cheers done at sporting events.

Clothing is a significant defining factor within the school environment. As Eckert notes, "[c]lothing and other forms of adornment, ways of speaking, territory, and even substance use and school performance all have symbolic value in the adolescent context."[16] Wearing all or part of a team uniform is one way the students physically expressed their group membership and group identity. This is a tradition on game days. In addition, wearing the uniform within the context of the school day marks certain students as not only belonging to the athletic group, but also as representatives of the school, having school spirit and being a part of the school community. The jocks and the cheerleaders, two of the most visible adult-sanctioned school groups, enjoy visibility and status within the school. Not only does this status mean being noticed in school, but it carries with it certain, more subtle rewards which will be discussed later.

Identification with the school culture and its administration, based on participation in adult-sanctioned activities, is one way to socialize students into corporate structures. High school, Eckert says, "provides a corporate setting through its strict delimitation of the corporate community, its isolation from the outside community, its internal hierarchical structures, its emphasis on role-oriented individual identity, and its task-oriented determination of interpersonal association."[17] Participation in adult-sanctioned and school-sanctioned activities, such as varsity athletics, not only mirrors a social reality that exists outside of the school culture but works as social capital within the school. Athletes are often given benefits or exemptions that other students are not afforded and some have come to expect these privileges from teachers even in cases where teachers are unwilling to extend the privileges.

For example, in a social studies class I observed frequently, Jaime complained to her teachers, Mr.Grey, about the grade she earned on a homework assignment. Jaime asked to be able to make corrections to the assignment and resubmit it for a new grade. Mr.Grey told Jaime that the assignment could not be done over. Hearing this, Matty, a popular basketball player, blurted out that Mr.Grey was being unfair and that as a cheerleader, Jaime has many extra-curricular responsibilities and is entitled to additional consideration on her homework assignment.

The fact that Jaime invests her time in the school as a cheerleader, Matty concludes, entitles her to academic privileges that other students do not receive. Matty's assumption that an athlete's service to the school can be translated into academic privilege is learned from the school culture and the additional considerations this system gives to those who actively participate in the adult power structure of the school.

In fact, when I was first observing in the school, I was surprised by the view that many of his teachers had of Matty. I witnessed Matty throw pencils at his teacher, disrupt class, walk out without permission during class and cheat on tests. Yet Mrs. Carson and Mr. Grey, in whose class he did all of these things, continued to view him as one of the "best students." Matty's status as an accomplished athlete and popular student was strong not only with his fellow students but with many of his teachers and in many cases this status appeared to translate into preferential treatment.

Eckert notes a similar pattern in the school she called Belten High School, where the students who identified with the adult-sanctioned school culture, which includes academic and extra-curricular realms, were rewarded with acceptance and popularity within the high school culture.[18]

The most visible rewards are those formally or informally given to students by faculty or the school administration such as early dismissal for those attending school events such as dances and general reluctance to punish behavior which for students of lower status would likely not go unpunished. The example of Matty's cheating in Mrs. Carson's class is a prominent one. Mrs. Carson was very strict about punishing those she caught cheating on tests and went to great lengths to expose (certain) cheaters in her classroom, even bringing in aides to observe on test days. However, her focus was continually on a limited group of students which did not include Matty. As an observer in the back of the classroom I could clearly view Matty and his friends pass crib sheets during tests. Due to my position as an observer and my reluctance to alienate my participants (a few of whom were Matty's friends) I did not feel it was my place to turn them in.

The less formal rewards which come from other students or the school culture are also significant. Athletes involved in the most popular sports at the school enjoy prestige within the school community. Informal privileges include community acknowledgement for the most popular sports and even local television coverage as well as the more common benefits of popularity within the school for those in the more prestigious cliques.

Within this setting of role-based privilege, the female athletes I spoke with talked about their dedication to both their extra-curricular activities and their academics. Many of the female students who were invested in extra-curricular activities also put forth effort in academic subjects. Excelling at both sports and academics was something I saw more frequently among the girls than the boys. In addition, many of these young women play more than one sport or participate in several school activities while also devoting time and effort toward their studies. Here, Jaime describes how much of her time is devoted to cheerleading.

> **Jaime:** *During the season, usually you have practice during the summer. You go to camp for four days. You have practice for probably about two hours a week, probably about four days. And*

then it gets more involved when you have football season, River Razz [a local football rivalry] and all that. It gets real involved. You go out to football games, cheer at those, you have practices, go to competitions. And then basketball season starts, you cheer all year and then try out again in May. We had try outs. And then it starts all over.
Carrie: What about softball, how much time does that take up?
Jaime: Softball is real time-consuming also. Our coach is real strict. He really works us to the bone. You have practice every single day except Sunday. Practices are usually two hours to two and half hours. You have a game usually about three or four times a week. Then we went to Florida for ten days over vacation. And you're expected to be at every practice on time and you can't miss [. . .]. It was all softball from the time you woke up to the time you went to bed.

In addition to her commitments to cheerleading and softball Jaime participates in many other extra-curricular activities. Besides playing bass clarinet Jaime participates in many school-sanctioned clubs.

Carrie: Are you in any other clubs here?
Jaime: Yeah, Outdoor club, I'm vice president. It's, like, a club to clean up the environment and stuff like that. In the community you go around and help out and stuff like that. You do, like, the beach clean up, you go tubing and whitewater rafting and stuff. And then I'm in World Connect. And that's a club for, like, the foreign exchange students, and you basically just talk about world issues, you go to trivia contests and stuff. I'm in Model UN, that's another club. Mr. Fletcher runs it. You talk about the UN and debates and issues and stuff like that. You go to a conference and you have a country and you have to hold up your placard and stuff. It's cool.

Alongside her many commitments, which also include a job as a hostess at a local restaurant, babysitting, and a relationship with a boyfriend who attends another school, Jaime also does very well on her schoolwork. She makes time for homework in the evening after her athletic practices and tells me her teachers would describe her as a "diligent worker."

Like Jaime, Chloe is involved in many school-sanctioned activities in addition to working at a coffee shop, altar-serving, and volunteer work with her church. One of her teachers described Chloe as "perfect." She is both a lacrosse and soccer player, and here, she talks about some of the other extra-curricular activities she is involved in.

Chloe: I'm involved with Outdoor club and Human Rights club a little bit.

Carrie: What do you do for Outdoor club?

Chloe: We go to cleanups and stuff like that, try to clean up the community a little bit. That's pretty much it. We do other stuff too, like fun stuff besides cleaning up the area. Like going tubing in the winter time and whitewater rafting was one of the things, too.

Carrie: What about Human Rights club, what do you do with that?

Chloe: Human Rights club, we fight for human rights and we're supposed to go and visit soup kitchens and stuff like that. But we do other stuff too.

Rachel discusses the time she devotes to her extra-curricular activities.

Carrie: How much time does that take up for you, on an average school day?

Rachel: With softball, there's practice every day for an hour and a half to two hours. Same thing with soccer [. . .] I usually have practice for soccer or softball, but if I don't, then I usually just go home and just watch TV or something. I don't like to do homework right after school because then, I don't know, I usually like to have a little bit of a break.

Carrie: Do your soccer or softball seasons overlap at all?

Rachel: A little bit, because softball sort of, like, goes into the summer. Like, softball is going to be ending this week or next week depending on how we do in playoffs, but my summer league for soccer starts this Thursday so I'm going to have to miss that game and maybe another one. But it's not that much of an overlap. And sometimes during the summer when I'm trying to do softball and soccer, it conflicts, like, the days and the times. I have to be there at the same time on the same day, and that conflicts and then I have to be, like, 'I'll go to the softball game this time, and I'll go to the soccer game next time,' you know.

Carrie: How do your coaches feel about that?

Rachel: Yeah, um, they're usually okay about it because they know that I like playing both sports, and I mean, I don't usually miss that many games, you know. If I miss one or two it's not usually that big of a deal.

Along with soccer and softball, Rachel devotes time to her studies and is an exceptional student. In the social studies class where I observed, she consistently had the highest test scores in the class and also tutors other students in math, her favorite subject, and plays the clarinet.

The intense level of involvement in school activities that Jaime, Chloe, and Rachel exhibit can be read as the girls' acceptance of the structured system of the school and its authority structures. In addition, the girls' visible participation in school-sanctioned activities works as cultural capital within the school with both teachers and students. Many teachers follow school sports and attend important games. Often, in class, teachers will compliment students, both boys and girls, for their performances during games. Students' participation in school sports and activities leads to a certain level of social acceptance and often adult approval, though participation is not the only factor in this acceptance and approval.

As mentioned, boys' football is the most popular sport at the school. The River City team has had a winning record for the year, and the games receive a lot of attention within the school and community. Like the cheerleaders, the football players wear their jerseys to school on game days, marking them as members of the team.

Ross tells me how he is defined by his football participation and his dedication to the team and the sport.

> *Carrie:* *How would you describe yourself?*
> *Ross:* *In certain words or what?*
> *Carrie:* *Any way you want to, certain things you're interested in or anything.*
> *Ross:* *Yeah, I hear I've got a pretty good personality and my, I'm pretty much driven by football. All my life is based around it . . .*
> *Carrie:* *So, what position do you play?*
> *Ross:* *I play offensive line.*
> *Carrie:* *How long have you been doing that?*
> *Ross:* *Well, I've been doing it forever, but on varsity since tenth grade.*
> *Carrie:* *And then, before that, you were playing in leagues outside of school?*
> *Ross:* *Ninth grade was JV and eighth grade was freshman. Before that, was NCA, which is little league.*
> *Carrie:* *How do you think your classmates would describe you?*
> *Ross:* *Some of them, the guys, would probably describe me as intense because of sports. And girls, probably as nuts.*

Ross perceives that there are different reactions from the boys and girls to the intensity he displays playing football.

One's participation in sports is a central identifying factor. Doug describes himself as both "normal" and notes that he plays "some sports," a factor that differentiates him somewhat and puts him into a separate category, beyond "normal."

> *Carrie:* *And where do you fit in?*
> *Doug:* *Kind of normal. I don't fit into, I play some sports.*

Dan describes himself in two ways; first as childish, next he adds athletic and later tells me about his athletic accomplishments.

> *Carrie:* *How do you think your classmates would describe you?*

> **Dan:** *Childish.*
> **Carrie:** *Childish, why?*
> **Dan:** *Because I do stupid things. And then I guess as athletic because I played football for, like, eight years. I played baseball, I played basketball. I always wanted to play hockey but it's too expensive. It's, like, one thousand dollars and then you've got to pay for the ice too, so.*
> **Carrie:** *Yeah?*
> **Dan:** *Otherwise, I would have really gotten into hockey. I was going to try out this season but I didn't.*
> *[. . .]* **Carrie:** *What are some things you like about this school?*
> **Dan:** *Sports. We've always had good sports, ever since I've been here. Football is the main sport that I play, and I've never had a losing year in football.*

Like Dan, many of the athletes are proud of their accomplishments and revel in the athletic success of the school teams. However, unlike the female athletes I spoke with, the males did not talk to me about their efforts to balance their homework and participation in sports. While most of the female athletes who spoke with me were also outstanding students, only a few of the male athletes excelled both academically and athletically, most excelling at sports rather than academics.

Being an athlete is meaningful for these students on many levels. Dan's story illustrates how the status that comes with being an athlete is interconnected with the power structures of the school. Dan is a football player who plays the role of class clown, often talking and making jokes in class. He is also experiencing many changes at home, as his parents are in the process of divorcing and his mother is pregnant. Though he tells me that he enjoys many of his classes, particularly American history, French, and German, and he wants to be a translator, he does not do well in school. Dan's talkativeness and failure to complete many homework assignments has led some of his teachers to become frustrated with him. His French teacher, Miss Teading, explains that she attempted to contact his mother, and she was unable to communicate with her because she does not speak English well. Dan's mother is originally from Germany where she met his step-father while he was in the military and stationed there.

As a result of Dan's declining grades and his "attitude problem," as one teacher describes it, Dan would soon be kicked off the football team. His failure to engage fully with the authority structure of the school and maintain his grades as well as display respect for his teachers led to his ousting.

While athletes are generally the more visible and popular students in the school, some of the less popular sports go virtually unnoticed. For example, until I conducted interviews, I was not aware that the school even had a bowling team or a golf team.

Alex is a shy and quiet girl in class. She tells me about her accomplishments as part of the school's bowling team.

> *Carrie: You also bowl, is that a school team?*
> *Alex: Yeah, at school. [. . .] We won the Snowdon tournament.*
> *They have all different kinds of tournaments, and we went to the*
> *Snowdon one and we got first place in that one, for the girls. And*
> *then, I think in championships we did, was it fourth? I'm not really*
> *sure about that one but I think it was fourth.*

Though Alex is a member of the school's bowling team, she is not marked in any visible way as an athlete in the school. Unlike the football, basketball, baseball, softball, lacrosse, soccer, and cheerleading teams, the bowling team does not visibly mark itself with uniforms worn during the school day. The team is also not a focus of student discussion during the school day, which accounts for the fact that I had not known of its existence until I interviewed Alex.

In addition, those in less popular sports do not construct their identities around their participation in the same way the football players or cheerleaders did. Many of the less popular sports and clubs, while officially representing the school, are not funded by the school and students often have to pay for their own supplies and uniforms. When asked to describe themselves, many of the football players immediately cited that they played football. For more than one of these boys football was a significant piece of his life, both in school and outside of school with his family and community.

While girls in other non-athletic school-sanctioned activities still reap some of the rewards of participation in the school culture, they are not able to claim the same level of visibility as the female athletes participating in more visible and popular sports. For example, Amanda participates in drama club.

> *Amanda: We put on a play,* Harvey. *A lot of people showed up,*
> *like, the first night, 130 people showed up. It was great—we sold a*
> *lot of tickets for a high school play. It was a great experience. I*
> *love theater. And I love what Amy Arturo has done for us at River*
> *City High School. She's amazing with theater and drama club and*
> *getting the clubs going. She's coming up with other clubs. It's*
> *great. The students here are really, they get into the school. And I*
> *love being with students, instead of going out on a weekend doing*
> *something totally destructive, they come here and they work on*
> *stuff that's in their interests.*

Despite the fact that this was a very successful school play, more so than past plays, Amanda did not receive the same level of visibility with her peers as do many of the female athletes. Her accomplishments were noted only by her peers and teachers who were close enough to her to know about her theatrical interests.

Eckert comments on the lesser status of arts in comparison to sports within high school hierarchy. "Artistic activities can play a role similar to that of athletic activities, but with the reservation imposed by the diminished value that American society places on the arts in comparison with sports."[19] The dominance of sports in high school, as both a reflection of the importance of sport in American society and as a school-sanctioned and school-promoted high status activity, stands in contrast to the attention, visibility and status given to other school clubs (whether arts-based, intellectually-based or activism-based). Even within the athletic system, the most popular sports (football, basketball, cheerleading, and baseball) overshadow other sports, as shown by both Amanda's and Alex's comments.

Here is what Dan, a seventeen-year-old football player, told me about cliques at River City High School.

> *Carrie:*   *How would you describe the people that go to school here?*
> *Dan:*   *There's a lot of groupings of kids. People aren't really super-open to everybody. They all have their little groups, like, that people are friends with. So, whatever group you look at is what you're going to see.*
> *Carrie:*   *What are the different groups?*
> *Dan:*   *Like, there's jocks or athletes. There's freaks, you know, like, smart kids and then it's just some of them are friends with each other but other than that it's mostly just groups of people.*
> *Carrie:*   *Where do you fit in?*
> *Dan:*   *I hang out with the football players because I play football and I have some friends that are smart kids but . . . .*

While Dan could place himself rather easily, due to his status as an athlete, not all students could, or were willing to, place themselves in the social hierarchy. Brian, a soccer player, talks about all the groups at the school and how he sees them.

> *Brian:*   *Like the people that I hang out with, they're great to hang out with and they're funny, they don't try be anybody else, you know what I mean?*
> *Carrie:*   *What are the different kinds of groups?*
> *Brian:*   *Like, you've got, there's preps [wearing preppy clothing], there's, there's gothic people [wearing black, clothing and sometimes dark makeup] here, there's, I don't know what you'd call them, people who, I don't know, like trying to be goth or something. Some people that drink, they just want to be on the sauce and don't care about anything else. And some people, like I know this one person who was a total prep and everything and then one day, out of nowhere he just flipped out, 'I'll be gothic!'*
> *Carrie:*   *So, where do you kind of fit in with all these different groups?*
> *Brian:*   *Like, it's not, like, I'm mostly friends with everybody. I can care less what they are. I don't know, if they have, like, piercings and everything, like their tongue or earrings. I don't care. And that's what a lot of people do do. 'He's not good enough' or what-*

ever. Like 'You're not so much a prep,' even if you wear Aero-
postale [brand of clothing]. 'You're not so much a ball player.'
You've got people like that. My one friend, he just wears whatever,
you know, it doesn't matter. Like, he'll wear, like, some really
bright color shirt, like green and then he'll wear a bright colored
orange shirt. It just doesn't matter to him.

Brian highlights how clothes work as semiotic markers of group status. His description of the ways different groups are identified includes dress, substance use, and
extra-curricular participation. Brian claims that, "I'm mostly friends with everybody." Observing him I noticed that, in school, Brian mainly associated with the
"smart kids" group. Outside of school, his time is dominated by his after-school job
and his girlfriend, who attends a different school.

Chloe was home schooled before ninth grade, when she started at River City
High School. She plays lacrosse and describes herself as belonging to "the more
quiet, friendlier group."

Carrie: How would you describe this school?
Chloe: How would I describe this school? Well, you definitely
have your cliques, so you've got the punk rock people and then
you've got the quiet people and then the popular kids. But it's a
pretty friendly school, I mean there's some good kids here and
[trails off] I don't know...
Carrie: Where do you fit in with those groups?
Chloe: Where do I fit in, probably I'm the more quiet, friendlier
group.

Aaron is a football player who wears "preppy" clothes and flaunts his image as
somewhat of a "bad boy."

Carrie: How would you describe the people who go to school
here?
Aaron: I don't know. There are a lot of differences, different
kinds of people, you know. I guess they're ok. They don't really
trash the school or anything.
Carrie: What are the different kinds of people?
Aaron: There's the athletic people and the freaks, kind of, I don't
know. Different kinds of people I guess.
Carrie: And where do you fit in?
Aaron: Average I guess, I don't know.

Aaron describes what he sees as diversity in the student body at River City. Many of
the students I talked to describe the River City High School as made up of many
different kinds of people and being "diverse." Frequently, the term diversity is used
to refer to racial, ethnic, or cultural diversity, and when I used this term in my inter-

views I had originally intended to speak of diversity in this way. However, I did not clarify my definition to the students and was surprised to find out that these white students did see their school as diverse and used the term diversity to refer to social diversity, or the presence of different cliques rather than racial, ethnic, or religious diversity.

Here, Rachel also talks about the diversity at the school. She tells me that the diversity at River City High School is one of the things that makes her school special.

> *Rachel:* There's a lot of different people, so some of my friends are different from other friends and they wouldn't be friends themselves but I can still hang out with them. The diversity of different kinds of people.
> *Carrie:* Like what kinds of people?
> *Rachel:* Some people are this kind or some people are like that. Like some of my friends aren't really athletic but I have friends who are from my soccer team or softball team.

When Rachel talks about diversity, she is not referring to racial or ethnic groups but to students with different interests and who belong to different cliques. As Perry notes in her work with upper-middle-class suburban white high school students, when there is a lack of racial diversity, other differences between students become pronounced and dominate the social structure.[20]

Joseph is also a football player who attended a public school in Northtown, a nearby larger city, before his family moved to River City.

> *Carrie:* How would you describe the people that go to school here?
> *Joseph:* Most of them are, you know, fun. There's always someone to talk to.
> [. . .]*Carrie:* And what are some of the groups?
> *Joseph:* There's the preps, there's the punks, there's the, um, I don't know. That's most of them.
> *Carrie:* Where do you fit in?
> *Joseph:* I guess I could be looked at as a prep, yeah.
> *Carrie:* What makes a prep?
> *Joseph:* I don't know, dress a certain way and you're with a certain group of people, so, you know.
> *Carrie:* So, how does school here compare to school in Northtown? Did you go to a private school or public school in Northtown?
> *Joseph:* Public school. There's a lot of different races in Northtown. There's a lot more ethnic backgrounds. A lot more languages.

The first aspect of Northtown schools that Joseph mentions is the "different races" and "ethnic backgrounds" found there. He contrasts this with River City where the population is racially homogeneous and presumably less ethnic, though many of the students do continue to identify with their families European ethnicities, at least verbally.

Maria talks about how athletics and football, in particular, dominate school culture during the season and serve as a way that students can identify themselves and each other.

> *Maria:* *The different groups of people, you've got your, like, you can always tell, when football season comes around because everyone kind of like, like, the football . . . there's cheerleaders, there's football players, like, you can kind of see who everyone identifies with. The other day, I said 'Who's your friend? Oh she's a soccer player.' A lot of things are identified with sports in this school because it's very big here. Like, there's cheerleaders, the jocks, I don't know what you would call them, the punky kids. I don't know what they want to call themselves. There are a lot of things identified with sports. You can always tell when the sports season comes around. Like, now it's baseball and everyone's into that so they identify with that.*
> *Carrie:* *Where do you fit in?*
> *Maria:* *I kind of, well I used to, I didn't try out for cheerleading this year but I was a cheerleader last year so that was a big thing. And I'm really going to miss that part of going to practice and having those people around me all the time. I mean, they're still my friends, we're still going to hang out and everything, but it probably won't seem that different. But they're going to be doing it and they're going to be talking about it, and I'm going to be there because I'm their friend and I'm going to be, like [trails off]*

Maria chose not to try out for cheerleading because of a fall-out she had with her coach resulting from her lateness to practice. As noted earlier, Maria's leaving cheerleading also coincides with a change in her family structure and possibly settled lifestyle as a result of her parent's divorce. For those who play sports, they identify themselves and are identified to others by this participation. As Maria points out, friendships develop around one's participation. She reflects on how her friendships might change when she is not a cheerleader next year and how she will miss "having those people around me all the time."

Both Maria's and Dan's families were in the process of possibly moving from "settled living" to "hard living." Maria and Dan (a football player whose mother was about to have a baby with her live-in "hard living" boyfriend) were both in the process of domestic change and possibly moving from "settled" lifestyles to "hard" lifestyles. Each family was not only changing in terms of its structure, but the economic futures for the families had become more uncertain with these changes. For the River City students, family stability and economic stability often went hand-in-hand.

Megan, who doesn't participate in any sports, offers a critical view of the jocks and the cheerleaders at River City High School.

> *Carrie: How would you describe the people who go to school here?*
> *Megan: Immature and petty. Very high school drama. They'll probably spend the rest of their lives with high school drama and never grow up from it. It's all about the cheerleaders and the jocks. You're nobody unless you're a rah-rah.*
> *Carrie: So, what are the different groups?*
> *Megan: You've got the jocks, the cheerleaders, the 'I don't cares' the nobodies, the stoners, the ridiculously dumb kids.*
> *Carrie: Where do you fit in?*
> *Megan: I'm the one, I don't care. I get along with everybody. I don't care to make friends, like, if I'm friends with somebody, I don't care, it ain't going to affect me tomorrow if I don't talk to them ever again.*

Megan uses the term "rah-rah" referring to jocks and cheerleaders, who in many cases had some economic resources with which they maintained their visible status. Name brand clothes such as Tommy Hillfiger and Abercrombie and Fitch worked as markers of status within the school.

Having a certain level of economic resources appears necessary to maintain a visible popular status. This would likely not even be an option for the poorest students, like Dana, who worked sometimes forty hours a week and contributed to her family's income. She had no time to participate in extra-curricular activities and probably few extra dollars to maintain a visible status. However, many of the students I interviewed who fell into the popular category (either by self-identification or as identified by others) came from "settled living" families who have economic stability. In addition, many of these students had jobs which gave them spending money and allowed them to keep up with the latest styles and, in some cases, pay for automobile insurance, gas, or associated expenses.

Megan, an outspoken critic of her schools' social hierarchy, equates popularity with money. While having some access to money may be a prerequisite for occupying the most visible positions in the school hierarchy, the stability of coming from a "settled" household versus a "hard living" one seems to be an even more significant factor in expanding a student's options. Hard living and settled living lifestyles, for the most part coincide with peer group membership and while there are examples of settled living students in a variety of cliques there are fewer examples of teens from hard living families in the most prestigious cliques.

Though some of the girls mentioned judgmentalism and racism as problems at their school, only one boy, Dirk, talked about this. Dirk tells me that he tries not to categorize people.

> *Carrie:* How would you describe the people that go to your
> school?
> *Dirk:* Judgmental.
> *Carrie:* Why is that?
> *Dirk:* I don't know, you get the occasional people that judge you.
> They're meeting you for the first time or what their friends say
> about you.
> *Carrie:* What are the different groups of people?
> *Dirk:* If I had to categorize them, it would probably be, like, foot-
> ball players, outcast kind of people, preppy. I don't know, there's
> popular and unpopular. I don't really categorize people.
> *Carrie:* Where do you fit within the whole spectrum?
> *Dirk:* I'm a floater.
> *Carrie:* You're a floater?
> *Dirk:* I just kind of go from one to the other, yeah.

Dirk connects his view of the cliques at the school and his negative experience on the
football team.

> *Carrie:* Do you participate in any clubs or sports or anything
> here?
> *Dirk:* I play lacrosse [. . .]
> *Dirk:* I tried football. That was too political.
> *Carrie:* Political? In what ways?
> *Dirk:* I don't know. I had the potential to start. Just because the
> one kid's name was a well-known name at River City, he was the
> starter. And it wasn't fun, they didn't make it fun.
> [. . .] *Carrie:* And you tried the football thing, what exactly hap-
> pened with that, you were on the team?
> *Dirk:* Yeah, I was on the team. But once they started, they had the
> starting line and then the second line. Once I was on the second
> line, I wasn't happy. I even had team members come up and tell me
> like, 'Why aren't you starting?' From there it went downhill be-
> cause once you get one bad move. It just wasn't a fun time.

Dirk quit the football team and took up lacrosse. He is up-front about acknowledging
the forces that kept him from starting on the football team and eventually led him to
quit. Though I have examined how certain cliques in the school are more aligned
with adult-sanctioned behaviors and activities than others, Dirk's comment illustrates
that these connections also weave into the larger social structure of the community.
Dirk's problems on the football team came in part from his unwillingness to accept
the social hierarchy that had already been established within the school and community which gave certain students and families higher status.

Nicole previously attended school in a nearby suburban district and compares her experiences there to her experience here at River City.

> ***Carrie:*** *How would you describe the people that go to your school?*
> ***Nicole:*** *Some I'd probably say . . . I don't know, our school's sort of like split up into groups, I guess you could say, like, a lot of schools. There's usually the smart people that are, like, geeks or something like that and the popular people, the semi-popular people. I guess I'd say probably there's, like, a half-and-half on, like, the stuck up and snotty people to the nice and I'd say half-and-half.*
> ***Carrie:*** *And where do you fit in in these groups?*
> ***Nicole:*** *In between.*
> *[. . .] If I could change anything, [it would be] the way that people view how they should be separated. For instance, how if you're not pretty or if you're not something, if you don't have the high standards or if you don't qualify for either one of them, you're put into a particular group. I think if I could change that and make people look more on the inside of the personality, I would probably do that. If the school weren't so racist and allow more variety of people like blacks and Chinese and that type of thing. That's about it.*
> ***Carrie:*** *Do you think those people aren't here because of the attitude here or . . . ?*
> ***Nicole:*** *That's what everyone says, I mean, like, in River City, and South River, you don't see many blacks living around here or Chinese. I think it's just maybe because the district—I don't know. Everyone thinks that River City's racist.*

Nicole is one of the few students to discuss the absence of other racial groups in River City. In her opinion, the lack of different racial groups is a result of the racism in the area and the fact that the whites do not allow diversity to exist here.

Conclusion

This chapter has discussed the ways in which students divide themselves, based on peer group membership, within the school setting and the extent to which these different peer groups identify with adult authority and "hard" or "settled" lifestyles. While this chapter has focused on the culture of the students and the students' perception of this school-based culture it is important to note that this culture does not exist in a vacuum. It is inextricably tied to the teachers, coaches, administrators and other adult and institutional cultures of the school. Neither does the school exist independently from the community or society. In many ways, the culture(s) of the students is a reflection of and reflects on the values and systems of the school and community as a whole. Yet at the same time as the students are a part of the system, some of them, for example Megan, Dirk, and Nicole, are able to critique what they see as the unfairness that is perpetuated by the hierarchical social system.

While race does not emerge as a site around which students separate themselves, the silence around whiteness is significant in this setting. In the next chapter I will continue this discussion as I reflect on the perceptions of whiteness as normalcy, as well as some of the economic divisions that emerge in conjunction with peer groups within the school.

Notes

1. "United States Census." 2000.

2. "New York State Report Card 2001–2002." 2002.

3. Perry, P. *Shades of White: White Kids and Racial Identities in High School*. Durham: Duke University Press, 2002. 106.

4. Eckert, P. *Jocks and Burnouts: Social Categories and Identity in High School*. New York: Teachers College Press, 1989.

5. Brantlinger, E. *The Politics of Social Class in Secondary School: Views of Affluent and Impoverished Youth*. New York: Teachers College Press, 1993.

6. Epstein, J. L., and N. Karweit, eds. *Friends in School: Patterns of Selection and Influence in Secondary Schools*. New York: Academic Press, 1983. 163.

7. Perry, P. *Shades of White: White Kids and Racial Identities in High School*. Durham: Duke University Press, 2002. 106; Eckert, P. *Jocks and Burnouts: Social Categories and Identity in High School*. New York: Teachers College Press, 1989; Brantlinger, E. *The Politics of Social Class in Secondary School: Views of Affluent and Impoverished Youth*. New York: Teachers College Press, 1993; Epstein, J. L., and N. Karweit, eds. *Friends in School: Patterns of Selection and Influence in Secondary Schools*. New York: Academic Press, 1983.

8. Davidson, A. L. *Making and Molding Identity in Schools: Student Narratives on Race, Gender and Academic Engagement*. Albany: SUNY Press, 1996; Dunphy, D. C. *Cliques, Crowds and Gangs: Group Life of Sydney Adolescents*. Cheshire: F.W. Cheshire Publishing Party, 1969; Perry, P. *Shades of White: White Kids and Racial Identities in High School*. Durham: Duke University Press, 2002.

9. Perry, P. *Shades of White: White Kids and Racial Identities in High School*. Durham: Duke University Press, 2002.

10. Brantlinger, E. *The Politics of Social Class in Secondary School: Views of Affluent and Impoverished Youth*. New York: Teachers College Press, 1993; Eckert, P. *Jocks and Burnouts: Social Categories and Identity in High School*. New York: Teachers College Press, 1989.

11. Brantlinger, E. *The Politics of Social Class in Secondary School: Views of Affluent and Impoverished Youth*. New York: Teachers College Press, 1993.

12. Eckert, P. *Jocks and Burnouts: Social Categories and Identity in High School*. New York: Teachers College Press, 1989. 22.

13. Brantlinger, E. *The Politics of Social Class in Secondary School: Views of Affluent and Impoverished Youth*. New York: Teachers College Press, 1993; Eckert, P. *Jocks and Burnouts: Social Categories and Identity in High School*. New York: Teachers College Press,

1989.

14. Weis, L. *Class Reunion: The Remaking of the American White Working Class*. New York: Routledge, 2004. 93.

15. Perry, P. *Shades of White: White Kids and Racial Identities in High School*. Durham: Duke University Press, 2002.

16. Eckert, P. *Jocks and Burnouts: Social Categories and Identity in High School*. New York: Teachers College Press, 1989. 49.

17. Eckert, P. *Jocks and Burnouts: Social Categories and Identity in High School*. New York: Teachers College Press, 1989. 103.

18. Eckert, P. *Jocks and Burnouts: Social Categories and Identity in High School*. New York: Teachers College Press, 1989.

19. Eckert, P. *Jocks and Burnouts: Social Categories and Identity in High School*. New York: Teachers College Press, 1989. 117.

20. Perry, P. *Shades of White: White Kids and Racial Identities in High School*. Durham: Duke University Press, 2002.

Chapter Five

"Normal" White Kids

Everybody is pretty much regular kids around here that I can see. There are some kids that are, that go above and beyond with their class work. There's just a lot of average kids here, that's all.

Ross—age seventeen

Peer groups, discussed in the last chapter, make up a part of the River City High School culture. Cliques are differentiated in semiotic and social ways, as well as by the different ways these peer groups align themselves with or distance themselves from the school authority and adult power structures of the school. The teachers, administrators, hidden curriculum, and peer interactions all play a role in how the students identify themselves within the school setting and within the larger social setting. At the same time as the students are constructing identities based on peer group memberships they are simultaneously constructing a larger group identity articulated through a dialogue of normalcy. This chapter discusses the ways the students within the school build their notions of whiteness and normality, and how they conceive of their place within the social system and the economy. These conceptions are then negotiated and renegotiated within the school setting and articulated in complicated ways.

Being White and Being Normal

Frankenberg explores the social construction of whiteness in *White Women, Race Matters*, describing whiteness as a "set of cultural practices that are usually unmarked and unnamed," as well as a structural advantage and a standpoint.[1] This description uncovers the many layers embedded in an identity which encompasses much more than a racial label. This complex and multilayered definition of whiteness is one which informs my own work, particularly the silences that exist in River City around whiteness and race.

Other work on the construction of whiteness has explored the ways it is constructed within different communities, particularly that of the white working class. This work finds that white group identities are constructed in relation to an "other," often a racial other, yet gender, sexuality, religion, and other factors all might play a role in this sort of identity construction.[2] This work highlights the fluctuation and changeable trajectories of racial categories exploring, for example, how certain

95

groups once categorized as non-white have become white.[3] Within racially homogeneous settings, such as River City, the topic of what it means to be white is one shrouded in silence and hinted at within a dialogue of "normalcy."

McIntosh discusses whiteness in terms of its privileged social position in comparison to others'. By conflating whiteness and privilege, McIntosh reveals the both subtle and pronounced ways that privilege is lived and experienced in everyday life. Central to McIntosh's argument is identifying spaces where power and privilege are present or lacking. She stretches to more fully understand the systems by turning her focus to the ways privilege works and, importantly, how it is both normalized and made invisible.[4]

Perry's study of white high school students and their racial identities discusses the complex ways that racial identity is conceived of and acted out within both racially mixed and racially homogeneous groups. Specifically important to my study are the observations Perry makes about the white students in a racially homogeneous environment. She discusses the importance of associations with others in identity formation. White students experienced themselves as normal and viewed race in general as an insignificant social or political category. In addition, these white students experienced what Perry refers to as a "cognitive gap" when trying to discuss white culture. These students, she also notes, were in most cases blind to the white privilege they experienced.[5]

Authors such as McIntosh, Frankenberg, and Perry point out some of the difficulties surrounding a discussion of whiteness. Their work highlights ways in which whiteness is interpreted as normal and the ways silence works to normalize whiteness, causing the invisibility of one's racial self while still marking the racial other. Building from the work of the authors discussed in this section, this chapter explores the silence and invisibility surrounding whiteness. Within this particular white working-class school, the construction of white identity is surrounded by a rhetoric of sameness and normalcy which identifies whiteness as the standard, or norm, and non-whiteness as deviating from that standard or norm. Paralleling Perry's example, the River City students also experience what she defines as a "cognitive gap" when discussing whiteness and were also generally unable to acknowledge the white privilege they experienced.

As stated, 98.5 percent of the students at River City High School are white. I asked the students at to describe the people at their school, and many of them answered that students at River City were "normal" or "regular kids."

Perry notes, "white people, by virtue of being members of the dominant group in this society, construct identities defined as 'normal' . . . To be defined as 'normal' means to not be defined at all, just to 'be.'"[6] In addition, being white is often identified as having no specific culture or being void of culture. White students at River City often describe themselves as well as people at their school as "normal" or "regular kids" and as they tell me this, they do not offer an explanation of what normal or regular means to them without prompting. There seems to be an assumption that the definition of normal is a shared one between us as white Americans, possibly strengthened by the significant time I spent in the school which also provided us with a shared context and points of reference for our conversations. When I asked students to elaborate on what they meant by terms like normal and regular the students would often struggle to articulate their answers, experiencing the "cognitive gap."[7] Their explanations then turned toward the differences that do exist within their social world, those expressed by cliques, dress, achievement, and gender, to name a few. Significant and visible among these are the cliques, which were discussed in the previous chapter.

Benjamin, a hockey player for River City High School's team, illustrates this identification of River City students and himself as normal as he describes the students who go to River City High School as mostly "the same."

> *Carrie: How would you describe the people who go to school here?*
> *Benjamin: I don't know, most of them are just the same, everyone seems to have their own lives and stuff. Everyone has their own pressure and stuff. [. . .] I mean, obviously, there's the people who, like, the kids who dress punky and shit. Not like they're different, that's just the way they dress, that's who they are. They have their own and I have my own friends. I'm sure everybody has the same pressures.*

Benjamin speaks a great deal about the pressures he feels from his family to do well in school. He assumes that his peers are also under the same pressures academically, although this was not the case within the group of students I interviewed. Unlike Benjamin, most students did not talk about intense parental pressures to do well in school. In contrast to information from upper-middle-class institutions, few River City students discuss concerns over striving for or maintaining good grades in order to get into college.[8] The non-conversant approach to college admissions displayed by the school culture is reflective of the less competitive schools that most students were applying to, such as the local community college.

Like Benjamin, a football player named Ross calls the students at River City "regular kids" and "average kids."

> *Carrie: How would you describe the people that go to school here? What kinds of different people are there?*
> *Ross: What kind of different people? Like groups of people?*
> *Carrie: Yeah.*
> *Ross: Um, Most of the kids, everybody is pretty much regular kids around here, that I can see. There are some kids that are, that go above and beyond with their class work. There's just a lot of average kids here, that's all.*

The students acknowledge that their peers are all similar and share the traits of "normal kids." Part of this assumption of normalcy is based in whiteness, a trait that in a racially homogenous group is not often discussed or questioned but exists as an unspoken, unifying factor.

Within this vastly racially homogeneous community, those few racial "others" stand out visually and culturally, but rarely speak directly about the racial assumptions that run as undercurrents in this school environment. Despite the predominant silence around race, my daily interactions with a Latino boy at River City made it apparent that he was acutely aware of his visible difference from his white peers. Alec is of Puerto Rican decent and participated in a preliminary survey I handed out in one of his classes. To the question "How would you describe yourself?" he replied with a one word answer, "tan." No white students responded by describing themselves by their skin color.

Doug, a football player, talks about the diversity at River City High School, yet refers to himself as normal. At the same time as he is employing the jargon of diversity, which was discussed in chapter four, Doug is also acknowledging his own normalcy among the groups of the school, in a way, refusing to place himself in its hierarchical structure.

> *Carrie: How would you describe the people that go to school here?*
> *Doug: It's pretty diverse. You've got your jocks and your punks—they're called freaks in this school. The jocks are into sports. Pretty diverse.*
> *Carrie: And where do you fit in?*
> *Doug: Kind of normal. I don't fit into . . . I play some sports.*

Though Doug does not identify himself as belonging to the jock category, he is a football player who socializes with other football players and cheerleaders, traits which caused others to view him as a jock.

Although claiming, or being claimed by the jock clique, provides its members with a certain amount of visibility and social capital within the school, other categories were associated with forms of social capital which were less powerful. For example, Bob had been labeled as belonging to the druggie group by both students and teachers who note his erratic behavior during classes as proof that he's "on something." Like Dirk, Bob claims that he does not categorize people who go to the school and he tells me that the students at River City are "just like everybody else."

> *Carrie: How would you describe people that go to school here?*
> *Bob: Just like everybody else.*
> *Carrie: Just like everyone else?*
> *Bob: Not the same but, I don't know how to explain it. Like, do different things. I don't know.*
> *Carrie: What about the different groups of people that go to school here?*
> *Bob: Like different groups, like, what do you mean?*
> *Carrie: Like people kind of divide themselves into different groups, groups of friends and things like that.*

Bob: I don't know. I guess. People say there are, like, preps and jocks and freaks and I don't know. I look at it, like, I don't really categorize people. I just do what I do.
Carrie: So, you don't feel like you fall into any of those categories?
Bob: Not really, no.

The expression of both normalcy and diversity articulated by these students at first seems contradictory. Perry mentions that race was rarely mentioned at Valley Grove (the mainly white and upper-class high school she studied) as it was not a dominant form of social organization there.[9] This is also true for River City, where non-racial forms of social organization are referred to when students talk about the differences that exist within their school culture. Overall the River City students view their peers and themselves as fitting a basic category of "American teenager," coded as white and ostensibly middle-class, a perceived class identity I will discuss later.

Not only do students see their own school setting and experience as being "normal" but some of them view all other schools as being like theirs. Discussing other schools, Rachel, sixteen years old, comments that she thinks all schools are pretty much the same.

Carrie: How do you think other schools differ from yours?
Rachel: I don't think it's really that different. Some people say that schools are so different, and I don't think that they are really that much different. Just the fact that they are a little bit smaller so that, you know, more people instead of being in a bigger school and not knowing everybody really well.

Alex agrees with Rachel that other schools are not different from hers.

Carrie: Do you think that their high schools are different from yours?
Alex: Probably in, like, bigger, bigger size and stuff like that. I don't think it's different.

This notion of normalcy, conflated with whiteness and a bureaucratic/working-class school experience (as defined by Anyon),[10] to Rachel and Alex, is a perceived universal, or at least American, norm. In an attempt to ferret out how students saw themselves in comparison to students at other schools, I asked them to compare their schools with other schools they may have knowledge of or be familiar with. Here is what Amanda has to say about how River City High compares to other high schools.

Carrie: How do you think other schools compare to RC [River City]?

> *Amanda: Really similar actually. When I went to all-county this year, because I had made it, at Waterville high school, there were lots of different school districts there. All different people, all different districts because you're the best in the county so you're going to have different people there. [. . .] They're just average people. Similar to here. It doesn't differ except that people think it does. People are like, 'Oh another school - it must be so much better than here.' It might be to start off with a clean slate if you've had a reputation. But if you didn't have a reputation in those schools, I don't know. If you're just yourself in those schools it's pretty much going to be the same thing. Pretty much, I mean getting to know different people—of course you have different lives. Everybody has their own individual life and that's what's so cool about meeting new people.*

Amanda describes the people who go to her school and other schools she has met as "just average people." Yet, at the same time, she contradicts herself by adding that her example is from a competition that involved the "best of the best." Amanda speaks to individuality as being the important distinguishing factor between people rather than group, school, ethnic or racial affiliation. The ideas she puts forth here fit the tone of her interview in which she expresses strong beliefs in meritocracy. Due to changes in her family structure, she has recently found out that her mother will not be able to pay for her college education. However, Amanda hopes that through hard work she can either get through college or make it to Broadway where she hopes to sing and act.

The population in River City has isolated itself from other racial groups in an almost wholly white community. Though quite a few teachers told me that there are more incoming students of color in the lower grades, over the last few years, the school district statistics show that all non-white populations combined still are not more than 3 percent of the entire student body. A look at the school district statistics shows the non-white student population (including Native American, Asian, Pacific Islander, African American, and Hispanic groups) going from only 1.6 percent in the 1999–2000 school year to 2.5 percent in the 2001–2002 school year.[11] So, while there has been an increase, this is only represented by a handful of students in each of the district's schools. Despite the extremely small number of students who make up this minority they are, however, a visible population since most are people of color.

Racially Coding "the City": Us and Them

Despite the fact that River City is only a short drive from Northtown, a large city, I only interviewed two students, Megan and Joseph, who spoke about traveling into the city regularly; Megan to visit her brother and boyfriend and Joseph to visit his grandmother. Sitting in on classes, I heard numerous derogatory comments about the city, Northtown, from faculty, staff, and students, many of these related to racial stereotypes. Often in discussions of Northtown the use of the term city was racially coded and becomes synonymous with African American.

One example of this I observed was as Mr. Ferell, a guidance counselor, visited eleventh grade classes to talk to students about applying to colleges. Here is a description of one of Mr. Ferell's visits to Mr. Grey's and Mrs. Carson's third period team-taught inclusion social studies class.

Mr. Grey begins by introducing Mr. Ferell to the class. Mr. Ferell then asks how many students in the class have taken the PSAT test, or pre SAT test. Six students raise their hands. He next asks, "How many plan to go to college?" and ten students, out of eighteen, raise their hands. "Wow!" Mr. Ferell exclaims, as if he is surprised by this number. Next, he asks, "How many plan to go right to work?" and two boys raise their hands.

Mr. Ferell then talks about the SATs and ACTs. He encourages the students who want to apply to college to take the ACTs because students at River City High, he tells them, tend to do better on the ACT than the SAT. He also notes that this test is now necessary for a lot of two-year, as well as four-year, schools. Mr. Ferell encourages juniors to sign up for "College and Career Information Day" as soon as possible since there are only two hundred spaces and there are around four hundred juniors.

Later, in the fifth period class, Mr. Ferell gives basically the same presentation. After passing out a packet of information he has put together on SAT preparation courses, he reviews the packet with the class. The first page lists free SAT courses given by a local university. Mr. Ferell warns the students, "I just want to alert you that there will be different types of populations there that you'll be exposed to." Though this SAT preparation class is free, he tells the class, "So, if you want to stay in the suburbs" and points the students toward the private test preparation companies. Mr. Ferell's statement reveals his assumption that River City students would be uncomfortable in a diverse learning environment. A free SAT course located in downtown Northtown could be expected to attract students from diverse racial, ethnic and economic backgrounds who live in the nearby area.

Traditional white working-class culture is one in which boundaries between racial, gender, and economic groups are firmly drawn and reaffirmed through cultural and structural forces.[12] By highlighting the differences between one's own group and "others," these boundaries are made and reinforced on a daily basis. As the economy and what it means to be working-class is changing, traditional working-class culture is adapting and changing also. As Weis points out many of these new working class families find themselves challenging traditional gender roles, in practice even if not consciously, in order to create economically stable lives for themselves and their families.[13] She notes that gender roles are being renegotiated as both men and women are working outside of the home for a wage while at the same time both are also working inside the home. The "settled living" working-class men and women find themselves sharing responsibilities like childcare. At the same time, other boundaries, such as those around race are being resolidified as the new white working class defines itself in opposition to other racial groups.

Within the River City High School community racial others were sometimes discussed formally and informally by students. Racial differences between River City and other places were pronounced, and antagonisms continue to exist and are highlighted in discussions of issues such as affirmative action and terrorism. I observed in a social studies class in which the teacher, who expressed awareness that she was teaching to a homogeneous white Christian group, sometimes used "us" and "them" terminology during lessons that included the histories of non-white peoples. For example, during a lesson on the Harlem Renaissance the teacher referred to white Americans as "us" and African Americans as "them."

Class Considerations

On one of my first days at River City I sat down to talk with one of the school's guidance counselors, Mr.Ferell, about the school. As I explained my project and my research questions he explained to me the class-based makeup of River City from his point of view. He noted that there were two types of families who lived in the River City district and whose children attended the public high school. From his office, he pointed out the window and told me that in one direction live the "white collar" families and the other way, the "blue collar" families. According to his directions the "white collar" section is made up of mainly newer homes, lots of well-kept ranch-style homes and a small neighborhood of larger homes in an older section of the city. A bit farther away, the "blue collar" side of town is made up of neighborhoods consisting of smaller homes and two-family dwellings interspersed with both open and closed offices, warehouses and factories.

The "blue collar" side of the city is not nearly so well kept. This side houses the bars, city buildings, and older homes. There is a small part of this older section of the city which has been slated for economic development and houses a few quaint looking shops, restaurants, and so forth, though it is far from the tourist attraction the city's website claims it will become.[14] This side of the city also houses numerous closed businesses and factories, some of which have been designated as hazardous waste sites.[15]

Mr. Ferell uses blue- and white-collar distinctions which highlight the changing economic experiences of the new working-class. The term blue-collar refers to manual labor jobs and the term white-collar, though unspecific regarding a job's level of autonomy, required education, or salary, does imply a non-physical form of paid labor. However, the distinction between blue- and white-collar is neither representative of class nor income differences. Nevertheless this distinction highlights a shift in the jobs available and the type of training or education needed to do these new types of jobs. As manufacturing, factory, and union jobs have become rarer in the area the workforce of River City has moved into service and skilled occupations, most of which require some sort of specialized training or education. The students' consensus that a college education is necessary reflects this changing reality of this economic setting.

Although Mr. Ferell frames his discussion of the local workforce in terms of "collars," the students do not use these terms, or class-based terms at all, to define themselves or their families. When asked to describe their families, most students again revert to the terms "normal" and "regular." A few also referenced their family's financial status as a point of difference between themselves and their peers focusing on the extras that a family with disposable income could provide, notably things like cars for their children to drive.

Megan talked with me about how she felt that having less money than some of her peers caused students to look down on her.

> *Megan: If you don't come from money you're nobody. And with five kids and my father owns his own business, I don't come from a lot of money, so.*
> *Carrie: Are there people around here that come from money?*
> *Megan: Yeah.*
> *Carrie: There are?*
> *Megan: I used to come from money until my mom and my grandparents got into a fight. We used to have a lot of money.*

Megan tells me about how she used to attend a private, Catholic school before her grandparents withdrew their financial support from her family. She tells me a little bit more about her family history.

> *Megan: My mom came from a very different kind of family than my father did. My dad's father was, like, working in factories and whatnot. He was in the Army. My mom's father, he was in the Army and all, but he was very into politics, he was very political. Their family, our family from Italy, came from money, though . . . Like, when my great-grandparents they were, like, the big-shots and the big-shot immigrants because they always had money, they didn't live in one of those apartments. They had, like, fifteen kids and they owned a home. It's not typical.*

In this discussion with Megan and similar ones with other students the nuances of a working-class culture become apparent. As noted, there are notable income differences within River City. Megan's family is an example of how cultural, economic, and ethnicity-based factors come together to produce a new working-class family identity.

Megan's father is the owner of a small construction business, allowing him a certain amount of autonomy at his work. His background includes serving in the Army and doing factory work. Megan's mother is from an immigrant family who was able to find a certain level of economic success (home ownership while supporting fifteen children) and pass some of this success on to Megan's family until a disagreement led Megan's grandmother to withdraw her financial help to the family. Although I do not know the family income, as Megan says, with a large family to support, despite her father's hard work there is not a lot of money for the family. Megan felt her family was not as financially stable as those of some of her cohorts.

Gwen, on the other hand, considers herself to be at the other end of the spectrum. She tells me she is "spoiled" by her parents, who allow her to drive their Cadillac to school and have promised her they will pay for her college education, even for a pricey private school if that is where she wants to go. Gwen describes herself.

> *Gwen: Perky. Cheerful. I'm a good friend. That's basically it. I mean, the classmates who like me [think this], the other classmates think that I'm a snob, I'm a spoiled brat, and stuff like that. I'm high class I guess. But I'm not.*
> *Carrie: Why do you think people think that?*
> *Gwen: Because my opinion on people is that if you don't have anything important to say to me and if I'm busy, then I have no time for you. But if I'm not, then I'll talk to you. [. . .] I'm not old enough to do it yet but I know what I want to do, so, I don't know. I'm a spoiled brat.*
> *Carrie: Why do you say that?*
> *Gwen: Because I get everything I want. Like, right now I'm driving my dad's 2001 Cadillac Catera.*

Gwen also acknowledges how hard her parents (referring to her mother and step-father with whom she lives) work to provide her family with all of these material things. Her step-father works at a local automobile factory and her mother works at a donut shop. Unlike Megan's family, this family exhibits a certain level of economic success with a car for Gwen to drive and luxuries such as frequent attendance at sporting events. The family's relative economic success leads Gwen to talk about having a greater choice of colleges than most of her peers. Although both spouses currently work full-time to maintain their successful "settled living" lifestyle, it is also significant that Gwen's mother struggled for many years after her first husband abandoned the family. It was not until she remarried that the family was able to enjoy this "settled" lifestyle Gwen talks about.

Despite the different financial standpoints of students like Megan and Gwen, there is a shared cultural capital, or shared cultural background, knowledge base, disposition, and skills which are passed from one generation to the next.[16] Each family relies on hard work to provide for themselves. Both girls also demonstrate this commitment to working hard: Megan works in a local bakery where she has been offered full-time employment and Gwen in a donut shop where she works with her mother and has also been offered a post-high school job. Though Gwen's family is now experiencing more financial success she shares an unacknowledged history of struggle with Megan, since both families have weathered economic ups and downs as well as changes in their family structures.

This shared cultural standpoint also functions to construct a view of the students' identities as normal, regular, and central. This, combined with the lack of racial and economic diversity in the River City community, positions the students to compare themselves to others who are racially and economically the same as them. In addition, the predominant media images of the outside world portray a version of average American culture as one which is white and ostensibly both middle-class and cultureless—though in reality it is neither.

Neoliberal discourses around individualism, consumerism, meritocracy and the naturalness of a free-market economy allow the River City students see themselves in stereotypical portrayals of American teenagers (read: white and middle-class). Apple explains, with the help of Menter et al., the neoliberal concept of capitalisms and its connection with the notion of meritocracy.

> They [markets] are said to be natural and neutral, and governed by effort and merit. Markets, as well, are supposedly less subject to political interference and the weight of bureaucratic procedures. Plus, they are grounded in the rational choices of individual actors. Thus, markets guarantee of rewards for effort and merit are to be coupled together to produce 'neutral,' yet positive, results.[17]

The easy availability of consumable culture, pushed by individualistic notions of choice disguised as freedom, further affirms this assumption. River City teens, many of whom work at part-time jobs and shop at discount stores like Wal-Mart and Target, can cheaply purchase the clothes they see in magazines and listen to the music they hear on the radio thus commodifying the identity of the American teenager. This commodification was further encouraged at school. For example, Mr. Grey encouraged his students to shop at Wal-Mart, touting it as "patriotic" and American to patronize this American-owned corporation.

Similar to the River City teens Willis's lads invested in clothing and entertainment as a way to express their adult status. However, in the case of River City students this investment additionally works to promote the idea that they are just like everybody else and by extension members of a middle class.

Placing themselves at the center of an ostensibly normal (white and perceived middle-class) world, the River City students are at a disadvantage for seeing their group as a part of the larger social and economic system. In fact, the River City High School students come from generally working-class backgrounds. Though higher education is now a viable option for them, most of their parents have not graduated from college and for this cohort it remains to be seen whether they will graduate from college. Many of them grew up in this formerly industrialized area, which only in the last fifteen to twenty years has lost its manufacturing base, which has forced its residents into alternative economic niches including many low-paying service and retail jobs for those not able to pursue further education or training.

With students presumably much like themselves as their main basis for comparison, the River City High School teens see themselves as average and arguably middle-class. Within this larger system and particularly in comparison to the middle- and upper middle-classes, River City can be considered somewhat economically and educationally disadvantaged. For example, using Anyon's model the educational culture of River City high school is a blend of both the working-class and bureaucratic examples of hidden curriculum which focus on rote memorization and direction following respectively and generally do not include creative or analytical thinking skills.[18] Instead, ideas about America being ostensibly middle-class, widespread belief in meritocracy, and the central yet invisible power of whiteness, wrapped in a discourse of normality, lead the River City students to view their social and economic location as the norm.

Positioning themselves as normal has potentially dangerous consequences on a number of fronts. It is in the realm of education, and higher education in particular, where we see the glaring differences between the working-class position of the River City students and the middle and upper classes. Ball et al discuss the class-based advantages that middle-class parents enjoy when dealing with the educational system.

> Middle-class parents are clearly the most advantaged in this kind of cultural assemblage, and not only as we saw because schools seek them out. Middle-class parents have become quite skilled, in general, in exploiting market mechanisms in education and in bringing their social, economic, and cultural capital to bear on them. 'Middle-class parents are more likely to have the knowledge, skills, and contacts to decode and manipulate what are increasingly complex and deregulated systems of choice and recruitment. The more deregulation, the more possibility of informal procedures being employed. The middle class also, on the whole, are more able to move their children around the system.'[19]

Most of the River City parents have little experience with higher education, and this, combined with sporadic guidance from the school, leaves the students at a distinct disadvantage when negotiating their higher education aspirations. For example, one student I spoke with (whose parents had not attended college) did not realize that the college application process should take place well before the end of her senior year and thereby missed deadlines for applying to colleges.

The discourse of normality works not only to blind the group to their economic disadvantages but also provides fertile ground for racism. By defining themselves as average or normal the River City teens have closed doors to a larger understanding of their economic standpoint, and in turn, this works to prevent them from viewing their individual economic and educational hardships as anything other than personal or family difficulties, stifling a larger class-based understanding of the struggles they experience. In addition, viewing one's own racial group as the norm and as central not only distances those who are different but creates an environment in which the concerns and issues of minorities can be dismissed.

Conclusion

This chapter has outlined how the River City High School students describe their racial and economic place in society as "normal." The term normal is loaded with racial and economic assumptions. Whiteness here is an unacknowledged and unquestioned norm, as communicated by the school and community. Surrounded by this, the River City teens have distinguished themselves within their racially homogeneous group using peer groups. These peer groups, in comparison with each other, create within the school culture what most students describe as diversity, while at the same time functioning as an internal critique of their similarities.

Along with the racial aspect of seeing themselves as part of a normal majority, most of the students view their school as the "same" as other schools. When talking about differences between schools, the students cite things like size and whether or not students are required to wear uniforms (as they are in many local private schools). Issues of resources and quality of education are not addressed or acknowledged. The perception of an average or central standpoint, heightened by the perceived equal access to higher education, allows the students to see themselves as ready to seize opportunities that may not have been available to their parents. While many of the students (in particular the girls) are aware of, and voice their concerns about economic and educational struggles, these are only on the level of "penetrations"[20] or "moments of critique,"[21] and not wholly realized class-conscious readings of an economically unsteady group that is struggling to define itself.

Striking in this chapter are the contradictions that emerge from what the students say about their everyday lives and their views of the world. Within this largely racially and economically homogenous space, the students employ a discourse of diversity, and within a working-class setting, the students are able to rhetorically place themselves within the context of a middle-class norm. Balancing these multiple considerations, the students create identities which reflect their understanding of the world, the authority structure of their school, and their social networks and embrace these contradictions. The students' identities and world views set the stage for how they approach their futures, and the ways in which they talk to each other, or the silences they create around the areas of race and class, in particular.

Notes

1. Frankenberg, R. *White Women, Race Matters: The Social Construction of Whiteness.* Minneapolis: University of Minnesota Press, 1993. 1.

2. Low, S. "Behind the Gates: Social Splitting and the 'Other'." In *Off White: Readings on Power, Privilege, and Resistance*, edited by M. Fine, L. Weis, P. Pruitt and A. Burns. New York: Routledge, 2004; Fine, M., L. Weis, J. Addleston, and J. Marusza. "White Loss." In *Beyond Black and White: New Faces and Voices in U. S. Schools*, edited by M. Seller and L. Weis. Albany: SUNY Press, 1997; Weis, L., A. Proweller, and C. Centrie. "Excavating a 'Moment in History': Privilege and Loss inside White Working-Class Masculinity." In *Off White: Readings on Power, Privilege and Resistance*, edited by M. Fine, L. Weis, P. Pruitt and A. Burns. New York: Routledge, 2004.

3. Brodkin, K. "How Did Jews Become White Folks?" In *Off White: Readings on Power, Privilege, and Resistance*, edited by M. Fine, L. Weis, P. Pruitt and A. Burns. New York: Routledge, 2004.

4. McIntosh, P. "White Privilege: Unpacking the Invisible Knapsack." *Independent*

School 49 (1990).

5. Perry, P. *Shades of White: White Kids and Racial Identities in High School.* Durham: Duke University Press, 2002.

6. Perry, P. *Shades of White: White Kids and Racial Identities in High School.* Durham: Duke University Press, 2002. 6.

7. Perry, P. *Shades of White: White Kids and Racial Identities in High School.* Durham: Duke University Press, 2002.

8. Kress, H. "Bracing for Diversity: A Study of White, Professional, Middle Class Male and Female Student Identity in a U.S. Suburban Public High School." dissertation, University at Buffalo, The State University of New York, 1996; Proweller, A. *Constructing Identities: Meaning Making in an Upper Middle Class Youth Culture.* New York: State University of New York Press, 1998; St. George, K. "Rethinking Reproduction: The Role of One Private, Catholic, and All-Girl High School in the Identity Development of the Young Women Who Attend." dissertation, University at Buffalo, The State University of New York, 2004.

9. Perry, P. *Shades of White: White Kids and Racial Identities in High School.* Durham: Duke University Press, 2002.

10. Anyon, J. "Social Class and School Knowledge." *Curriculum Inquiry* 11, no. 1 (1981): 3–42.

11. "New York State Report Card 2001–2002." 2002.

12. Willis, P. *Learning to Labor: How Working Class Kids Get Working Class Jobs.* New York: Columbia University Press, 1977; Weis, L. *Working Class without Work: High School Students in a Deindustrializing Economy.* New York: Routledge, 1990.

13. Weis, L. *Class Reunion: The Remaking of the American White Working Class.* New York: Routledge, 2004.

14. www.rivercity.org. River City.org is a pseudonym used to protect the identities of the participants.

15. River City News, 2002. River City News is a pseudonym.

16. Bourdieu, P. "Structures, Habitus, Practices. "In *Social Theory: The Multicultural and Classic Readings*, edited by C. Lemert. Boulder: Westview Press, 1993.

17. Menter et al. in Apple, M. "omparing Neo-Liberal Projects And Inequality in Education." *Comparative Education* 37, no. 4 (2001): 409–23. 413.

18. Anyon, J. "Social Class and School Knowledge." *Curriculum Inquiry* 11, no. 1 (1981): 3–42.

19. Ball et al. in Apple, M. "Comparing Neo-Liberal Projects And Inequality in Education." *Comparative Education* 37, no. 4 (2001): 409–23. 415.

20. Willis, P. *Learning to Labor: How Working Class Kids Get Working Class Jobs.* New York: Columbia University Press, 1977. Willis describes "penetrations" as moments in which the working class "sees through" the reproductive aspects of the social and economic system. However, these do not lead to an overall class-based critique.

21. Weis, L. *Working Class without Work: High School Students in a Deindustrializing Economy.* New York: Routledge, 1990. Weis describes "critical moments of critique" as they exhibit a critique of male dominance and patriarchy which falls short of a collective struggle.

Chapter Six

Conclusions

This study was undertaken in order to follow up on the stories of working-class adolescents in the new millennium. Guided by the following research questions, I discuss the multiple ways that white, working-class youth construct their identities in a changing social and economic context.

- How do white working-class youth in a large urban high school construct their identities with and against the social, academic, and extracurricular areas of the school?
- What are the students' articulated relationships with other groups and agencies outside of the school, such as families, churches, and places of employment?
- In what ways do these identities relate to perceptions of their future roles with respect to education, occupation, and family?

Examining these aspects of identity construction allows for a discussion of the multiple factors which the students use to make sense of their lives.

Chapter Two—Girls at River City High School—explores girls' lives through their own words. Their relationships with their families and their mothers, in particular, came to light as important to the girls' conceptions of themselves and their futures. Particularly striking are the stories of their mothers, many of whom were struggling with education, employment, and family situations. Contrary to popular conceptions which situate white girls as distanced from their mothers, the River City girls expressed intense identification and empathy with their mothers, particularly around histories of struggle. For many of the girls these histories and sometimes current situations functioned as life-lessons that the girls were able to refer to when thinking about their own future plans.

In 1990, Weis described working-class girls who were experiencing "moments of critique" in which they critiqued the patriarchal system and challenged traditional gender roles. These moments of critique frequently resulted in the girls considering futures that foregrounded independence.[1] Traditional heterosexual relationships, which once were central to working-class girls' identities and financial stability were no longer foregrounded in these critiques.[2] The girls at River City have developed the moment of critique into a view of their own positions which foreground education and financial independence and include plans for marriage and/or family which often take a backseat to independence and stability.

Traditional gender roles are being reworked, in practice if not in theory also, by many of the parents, and mothers, in particular, of the River City students. Many of the mothers are facing challenges in their lives which leave them struggling for financial and familial stability. Education and employment are viewed as two possible routes to obtaining financial stability. Their daughters both identify and empathize with the struggles of their mothers. They translate this experience into a need for financial independence, which many see as dependent on educational credentials.

The intense identification River City girls experience with their mothers and their struggles is juxtaposed with the absence of identification the boys exhibit. Unlike the girls, River City boys occasionally acknowledge their mothers' struggles but do not relate them to their own future plans or conceptions of gender relations. The boys struggle to carve out a new version of white working-class masculinity as they wrestle with ideas about traditional gender roles and family structures, even as their female cohorts envision a separate level of independence. Instead of responding with identification and empathy, the boys respond to family struggles with sympathy articulated as a respect for their mothers' hard work, a desire to protect them, and most important a desire to attain a settled lifestyle, often through a reinterpretation of traditional white working-class masculinity which includes a significant domestic role for men.

This difference in how boys and girls interpret and apply lessons from their family situation points toward a renegotiation of traditional white, working-class gender roles and is documented by Weis.[3] Her study finds that women's roles are changed in fundamental ways as they contribute more economically to their households than in the past. One of the ways they do this is through education, which puts the women in a position to contribute more money to their households. When both men and women work outside of the home, wholly traditional divisions of labor are no longer practical or sometimes even possible. Weis found that white working-class men, to some extent, are stepping in to fill in gaps with regard to child care and household chores. Though this change is documented in the households of working-class adults now in their thirties, it was not a future that the men, in particular, envisioned for themselves as high school students.

In the River City example, boys do not talk about the changes in gender roles they see around them (though from the girls' interviews I have concluded that in many cases these shifts are present in families). The changing dynamics within working-class families, where both women and men often work outside of the home for a wage, is embraced by necessity by the River City girls. In addition, the girls acknowledge the possibility of divorce and single parenthood. The boys, while aware of the reality of divorce (though possibly not single parenthood for themselves), do not personally feel pressures to guard themselves against these realities and prepare for a variety of family life possibilities as the girls do.

Although the boys do not widely internalize a need to change their role within the family, it is possible that this might change as they find themselves partnering up in families, particularly heterosexual couples in which women work full-time outside of the home. The boys, however, do articulate the need for education, in contrast to older generations of working-class boys.[4] The reality of the deindustrialized economy and particularly tight and changing job market in River City and the surrounding area force the boys to think about new possibilities for employment.

On the economic front, the River City boys, almost unanimously, plan to pursue higher education. By and large, as the boys discuss their plans their reasoning focuses more on opportunity than the pressing necessity that was the focus for the girls. These differences highlight two standpoints from which the educational system and economy is observed in significantly different ways. As the girls critique their social/family location (though, as noted in Chapter Two this falls short of a class- or gender-based critique and instead rests at the level of family) the boys adopt a somewhat more neoliberal stance, viewing themselves as poised to take advantage of their educational options. The boys' impetus for taking advantage of these options comes out of a perceived necessity. The discussion of this necessity is based in an "everybody else is doing it" kind of competitive approach rather than a fear of economic struggle.

Family, educational, and career experiences and possibilities are negotiated by the River City students every day. An important site for this negotiation is the school where students spend a good deal of their time and construct their identities as members of larger groups. The student culture of River City presents students with opportunities to further create and solidify their identities, specifically in relation to those like them and in contrast with others. Literature on school cultures tells us that group identities are often formed around racial groups.[5] Over time and place, the definitions and meanings behind specific racial categories have changed, but in recent years the term "white" in the United States has come to be used for most Americans of European descent, as well as other groups of similar skin-color appearance. Within the River City community, which is largely racially homogeneous, the students divide themselves along other lines: gender (explored in Chapters Two and Three), ethnic heritage (to some extent – though not discussed in this work), and peer groups (being the most salient in this environment).

Chapter Four explores peer groups and the ways that River City High School students identify themselves and/or are identified by others as members of these groups. Those students who participate heavily in school-sponsored activities identify most closely with the authority system of the school. Students who do not identify with the school's official authority are most often the students who do not participate in school-sponsored activities.[6] Other parallels can be drawn between school cliques and "hard living" and "settled living" families. The "settled" lifestyle affords students a level of opportunity to be a part of the more prestigious and visible school cliques, which at River City High School generally revolve around athletic involvement.

Chapter Five further investigates the ways white River City students construct their identities as members of a distinct yet unnamed racial group. Perry's study of whiteness explores ways large, racially homogeneous groups use non-racial factors as ways to conceive of difference.[7] At River City, the white population divides itself using peer groups (Chapter Four) and many students additionally identify themselves by the ethnic group with which they and their families most closely identify. For example, students identify as Irish, Italian, Polish, etc., though these labels are rarely applicable as group identities within school but are instead rhetorically articulated by individuals and probably more salient in the family setting. These markers of difference are read by many students as "diversity" just as the peer groups themselves are also read as representing a diverse community.

Complicating their dialogues of diversity is the students' identification of themselves as "normal" which is elaborated on in Chapter Five. The perception of being normal and like everybody else promotes the notion that their school, family, and life experiences are central to, and representative of, a sort of generic American life. I discuss the ways that this standpoint, at the same time as it positions students to take advantage of higher education, also works to obscure their educational and economic disadvantages and decenters issues of difference, most significantly, race and class.

Open Questions

This work provides a description of the identity formation of white working-class girls and boys in a particular deindustrialized area of the Northeast. While the data presented here is not necessarily generalizable, it does open a door for understanding some of the difficulties and issues that confront this group of students and also presents us with an example of social and economic change and the multiple considerations that face a young generation about to embark on a relatively new path for their class.

The study raises many questions about the future of the white working class. Situated in a changing economy, we have seen this group reposition itself over the past two decades.[8] This repositioning means more than simply attending college: it means developing new ways to think about occupations, class, and gender roles both inside and outside of the home. It also has significant political consequences as the working class, poised between the middle class and the poor, attempts to redefine itself culturally as a middle-class group while fighting the declining value of a college credential, the tight job market (in which low-paying service jobs are plentiful, health insurance is fast becoming unaffordable for working families, and the gap between a minimum wage and a living wage is growing) and confronting changing domestic roles.

The data show that there are still some tensions between older working-class roles and new educational, occupational, and gender roles. These tensions are sometimes verbally articulated and sometimes ignored, but they play out in the schools, and the lives of the adolescent girls and boys with whom I spoke. Significantly, the girls and boys are often approaching these issues in different ways.

The girls, who focused on their desire for economic independence, which for the most part grew out of their personal experiences and signals from family members, expressed concerns about being able to support themselves, and possibly future children. Though they did not necessarily exclude partners from their future plans, many of the girls wanted the option of being self-sufficient, regardless of whether or not they had a partner. This expressed desire is well intentioned but not supported by the literature, which illustrates the necessity for dual-earner households, even for those with a college education.[9]

> Through the last quarter of the twentieth century [in the United States], family incomes remained nearly unchanged despite falling wages. This was possible only because the number of wage earners in the average family increased sharply, especially for families with children at home . . . Between 1972 and 1992, the percentage of 'traditional families' (Dad working, Mom at home with the kids) fell from 23 percent of all U.S. families to 9 percent.[10]

Weis's work illustrates how this has happened on a more personal level for white working-class families in her conversation about "settled living" families who have been able to attain a stable lifestyle through the dual income household and dual domestic participation.[11]

The girls in this study who talk about protecting themselves against these struggles may be disappointed to find that their hard work will not guarantee them a comfortable independence, particularly if they choose to have children.

One of the more striking findings from these interviews was that so many, in fact almost all, of the students I interviewed planned to go to college. Upon further examination, their dialogues illustrate the ways they are approaching higher education in a way which reflects some of the limitations they face coming from a working-class standpoint. These students are not, for the most part, pursuing the "college experience" that includes living on campus, participating in student life, and finding themselves. Instead, many of them want to live at home and express a greater interest in the value of the degree than the experience as a whole. This may not be a limitation so much as a class-based response to higher education that has been developed by the River City students through their interactions with their families, peers, and school culture.

Another aspect of this group's standpoint pertaining to higher education is that so many of them plan to work their way through college, making enough money to pay their tuition and support themselves. This is combined with an overall reluctance to take student loans and put their families into debt. This is a message directly given to them by their guidance counselors and teachers as well as more subtly embedded in their cultural experience. While there certainly are good arguments for not taking loans to get through school, the position that if a student cannot make or save enough money for college he or she should not attend will likely lead to many working-class students dropping out or taking additional time to finish their educations. In addition, there will likely be negative academic consequences for those students who attempt to work enough to pay their bills and carry a full course load.[12] I am not advocating that this approach to college education is wrong or right, but illustrating the approach toward education that this group of students is constructing.

Also discussed is the overall lack of understanding the River City students have of the higher education hierarchy. This factor plays into the above conclusions, as well. What I have termed a lack of understanding may also function as a protective mechanism for these students. By not selecting the most challenging colleges and universities, these students are poised to have a college experience for which they may be better prepared. For example, the popular choice of the local community college is one where many of the River City students are told they will succeed. In fact, the community college is connected with the high school and some of the courses overlap (for example, vocational courses) and in some ways work as extensions of their high school education.

Around the issue of higher education, questions about equal access and opportunity for working-class students surface as a result of this research. As this work illustrates, there are systemic and economic factors at work that move the students toward community colleges and other local, accessible institutions for extremely practical reasons. These are the students who do not experience many options when thinking about higher education and their experiences highlight the need for affordable, accessible, and quality higher education options.

Zweig, who defines class as a group's relationship to power, and particularly how much power a group has within and over their work, argues that "[t]he working class is 62 percent of the labor force."[13] Overall, there is a great deal to consider about the ways working-class adolescents are transitioning into adulthood and the ways they will shape the new white working class. Within a society that virtually denies the existence of class altogether, it is important to understand the dynamics of power as they are played out in the lives of those who are the workers with the least power in the hierarchy. This work has attempted to break off a piece of these larger social and economic issues to reach an understanding of how this white working-class fraction is being defined and defining itself in the new millennium.

Notes

1. Weis, L. *Working Class without Work: High School Students in a Deindustrializing Economy.* New York: Routledge, 1990. Weis describes "critical moments of critique" as they exhibit a critique of male dominance and patriarchy which falls short of a collective struggle.

2. McRobbie, A. "Working Class Girls and the Culture of Femininity." In *Women Take Issue: Aspects of Women's Subordination,* edited by CCCS. London: Hutchinson, 1978.

3. Weis, L. *Class Reunion: The Remaking of the American White Working Class.* New York: Routledge, 2004.

4. Willis, P. *Learning to Labor: How Working Class Kids Get Working Class Jobs.* New York: Columbia University Press, 1977; Weis, L. *Working Class without Work: High School Students in a Deindustrializing Economy.* New York: Routledge, 1990.

5. Perry, P. *Shades of White: White Kids and Racial Identities in High School.* Durham: Duke University Press, 2002; Willis, P. *Learning to Labor: How Working Class Kids Get Working Class Jobs.* New York: Columbia University Press, 1977; Weis, L. *Working Class without Work: High School Students in a Deindustrializing Economy.* New York: Routledge, 1990.

6. Eckert, P. *Jocks and Burnouts: Social Categories and Identity in High School.* New York: Teachers College Press, 1989.

7. Perry, P. *Shades of White: White Kids and Racial Identities in High School.* Durham: Duke University Press, 2002.

8. Dolby, N., and G. Dimitriadis, eds. *Learning to Labor in New Times*. New York: RoutledgeFalmer, 2004; Reich, R. *I'll Be Short: Essentials for a Decent Working Society*. Boston: Beacon Press, 2002; Zweig, M. *The Working Class Majority: America's Best Kept Secret*. Ithaca: Cornell University Press, 2000.

9. Ehrenreich, B. *Nickel and Dimed: On (Not) Getting by in America*. New York: Metropolitan Books, 2001; Reich, R. *I'll Be Short: Essentials for a Decent Working Society*. Boston: Beacon Press, 2002; Weis, L. *Class Reunion: The Remaking of the American White Working Class*. New York: Routledge, 2004; Zweig, M. *The Working Class Majority: America's Best Kept Secret*. Ithaca: Cornell University Press, 2000.

10. Zweig, M. *The Working Class Majority: America's Best Kept Secret*. Ithaca: Cornell University Press, 2000.

11. Weis, L. *Class Reunion: The Remaking of the American White Working Class*. New York: Routledge, 2004.

12. Carr, R., Wright, J., & Brody, C. "Effects of High School Work Experience a Decade Later: Evidence from the National Longitudinal Survey." *Sociology* 69. no. 1 (1996); Bloom, J. "Hollowing the Promise of Higher Education: Inside the Political Economy of Access to College." In *Beyond Silenced Voices: Class, Race and Gender in United States Schools*, edited by L. Weis and M. Fine. Albany: SUNY Press, 2005.

13. Zweig, M. *The Working Class Majority: America's Best Kept Secret*. Ithaca: Cornell University Press, 2000.

Bibliography

Anyon, J. "Social Class and School Knowledge." *Curriculum Inquiry* 11, no. 1 (1981): 3-42.
Apple, M. "Comparing Neo-Liberal Projects And Inequality in Education." *ComparativeEducation* 37, no. 4 (2001): 409–23.
Bloom, J. "Hollowing the Promise of Higher Education: Inside the Political Economy of Access to College." In *Beyond Silenced Voices: Class, Race and Gender in United States Schools*, edited by L. Weis and M. Fine. Albany: SUNY Press, 2005.
Bluestone, B., and B. Harrison. "The Deindustrialization of America: Plant Closings, Community Abandonment, and the Dismantling of Basic Industry." New York: Basic Books, 1982.
———. *Growing Prosperity: the Battle for Growth with Equity in the Twenty-First Century.* Boston: Houghton Mifflin Company, 2000.
Bogdan, R., and S. K. Bicklin. *Qualitative Research for Education: An Introduction to Theory and Methods.* Boston: Allyn and Bacon Inc., 1982.
Bourdieu, P. "Structures, Habitus, Practices." In *Social Theory: The Multicultural and Classic Readings*, edited by C. Lemert. Boulder: Westview Press, 1993.
Bowles, S., and H. Gintis. *Shooling in Capitalist America: Educational Reform and the Contradictions of Economic Life.* New York: Basic Books, 1976.
Brantlinger, E. *The Politics of Social Class in Secondary School: Views of Affluent and Impoverished Youth.* New York: Teachers College Press, 1993.
Brodkin, K. "How Did Jews Become White Folks?" In *Off White: Readings on Power, Privilege, and Resistance*, edited by M. Fine, L. Weis, P. Pruitt and A. Burns. New York: Routledge, 2004.
Carr, R., J. Wright, and C. Brody. "Effects of High School Work Experience a Decade Later: Evidence from the National Longitudinal Survey." *Sociology* 69, no. 1 (1996).
Davidson, A. L. *Making and Molding Identity in Schools: Student Narratives on Race, Gender and Academic Engagement.* Albany: SUNY Press, 1996.
Dolby, N., and G. Dimitriadis, eds. *Learning to Labor in New Times.* New York: RoutledgeFalmer, 2004.
Dunphy, D. C. *Cliques, Crowds and Gangs: Group Life of Sydney Adolescents.* Cheshire: F.W. Cheshire Publishing Party, 1969.
Eckert, P. *Jocks and Burnouts: Social Categories and Identity in High School.* New York: Teachers College Press, 1989.
Ehrenreich, B. *Nickel and Dimed: On (Not) Getting by in America.* New York: MetropolitanBooks, 2001.
Epstein, J. L., and N. Karweit, eds. *Friends in School: Patterns of Selection and Influence in Secondary Schools.* New York: Academic Press, 1983.
Fine, M., L. Weis, J. Addleston, and J. Marusza. "White Loss." In *Beyond Black and White: New Faces and Voices in U. S. Schools*, edited by M. Seller and L. Weis. Albany: SUNY Press, 1997.
Finn, P. J. *Literacy with an Attitude: Educating Working-Class Children in Their Own Self Interest.* Albany: SUNY Press, 1999.

Fordham, S. "'Those Loud Black Girls' (Black) Women, Silence, and Gender 'Passing' in the Academy." In *Beyond Black and White: New Faces and Voices in U.S. Schools*, edited by M. Seller and L. Weis. Albany: SUNY Press, 1997.

Frankenberg, R. *White Women, Race Matters: The Social Construction of Whiteness*. Minneapolis: University of Minnesota Press, 1993.

Gaines, D. *Teenage Wasteland: Suburbia's Dead End Kids*. Chicago: University of Chicago Press, 1998.

Gaskell, J. "Gender and Course Choice: The Orientation of Male and Female Students." *Journal of Education* 166 (1984): 89–102.

———. *Gender Matters: From School to Work*. Philadelphia: Open University Press, 1992.

"Hazardous Waste Sites in Our County." *River City South News* 2000.

Hochschild, A. *The Second Shift*. New York: Penguin Books, 2003.

Holland, D., and M. Eisenhart. *Educated in Romance: Women, Achievement, and College Culture*. Chicago: University of Chicago Press, 1990.

Imms, W. "Multiple Masculinities and the Schooling of Boys." *Canadian Journal of Education* 25, no. 2 (2000): 152–65.

Keister, L. *Wealth in America: Trends in Wealth Inequality*. Cambridge: Cambridge University Press, 2000.

Kenny, L. D. *Daughters of Suburbia: Growing up White, Middle Class, and Female*. New Brunswick: Rutgers University Press, 2000.

Kress, H. "Bracing for Diversity: A Study of White, Professional, Middle Class Male and Female Student Identity in a U.S. Suburban Public High School." dissertation, University at Buffalo, The State University of New York, 1996.

Low, S. "Behind the Gates: Social Splitting and the 'Other'." In *Off White: Readings on Power, Privilege, and Resistance*, edited by M. Fine, L. Weis, P. Pruitt and A. Burns. New York: Routledge, 2004.

Mac an Ghaill, M. *The Making of Men: Masculinities, Sexualities and Schooling*. Buckingham: Open University Press, 1994.

MacLeod, J. *Ain't No Makin' It: Aspirations and Attainment in a Low-Income Neighborhood*. Boulder: Westview Press Inc., 1995.

Mantsios, G. "Class in America - 2003." In *Race, Class and Gender in the United States: An Integrated Study*, edited by P. Rothenberg. New York: St. Martin's Press, 2004.

McIntosh, P. "White Privilege: Unpacking the Invisible Knapsack." *Independent School* 49 (1990).

McLaren, P., and V. Scatamburlo-D'Annibale. "Paul Willis, Class Consciousness, and Critical Pedagogy: Toward a Socialist Future." In *Learning to Labor in New Times*, edited by N. Dolby and G. Dimitriadis. New York: RoutledgeFalmer, 2004.

McRobbie, A. "Working Class Girls and the Culture of Femininity." In *Women Take Issue: Aspects of Women's Subordination*, edited by CCCS. London: Hutchinson, 1978.

Millls, R., and S. Bhandari. "Health Insurance Coverage in the United States: 2002." edited by Economics and Statistics Administration U.S. Department of Commerce: U.S. Census Bureau, 2003.

"New York State Report Card 2001–2002." 2002.

Oakes, J. *Keeping Track: How Schools Structure Inequality*. New Haven: Yale University Press, 1985.

Orenstein, P. *Schoolgirls: Young Women, Self-Esteem, and the Confidence Gap*. New York: Anchor Books, 1995.

Perry, P. *Shades of White: White Kids and Racial Identities in High School*. Durham: Duke University Press, 2002.

Pipher, M. *Reviving Ophelia: Saving the Selves of Adolescent Girls*. New York: Ballatine

Books, 1994.

Proweller, A. *Constructing Identities: Meaning Making in an Upper Middle Class Youth Culture*. New York: State University of New York Press, 1998.

Region's Largest Employers. 2004. In Local Development Association. (accessed 2004).

Reich, R. *I'll Be Short: Essentials for a Decent Working Society*. Boston: Beacon Press, 2002.

———. *The Work of Nations: Preparing Ourselves for 21st Century Capitalism*. Albany: SUNY Press, 1997.

Rubin, L. *Families on the Fault Line: America's Working Class Speaks About the Family, the Economy, Race and Ethnicity*. New York: Harper Collins, 1994.

———. *Worlds of Pain: Life in the Working-Class Family*. New York: Basic Books, 1976.

Sklar, H. *Chaos of Community: Seeking Solutions, Not Scapegoats for Bad Economics*. Boston: South End Press, 1995.

Sklar, H., L. Mykyta, and S. Wefald. *Raise the Floor: Wages and Policies That Work for All of Us*. New York: Ms. Foundation for Women, 2001.

St. George, K. "Rethinking Reproduction: The Role of One Private, Catholic, and All-Girl High School in the Identity Development of the Young Women Who Attend." dissertation, University at Buffalo, The State University of New York, 2004.

"United States Census." 2000.

Walkerdine, V., H. Lucey, and J. Melody. "Growing up Girl: Psychological Explorations of Gender and Class." In *Off White: Readings on Power, Privilege and Resistance*, edited by M. Fine, L. Weis, P. Pruitt and A. Burns. New York: Routledge, 2004.

Weiler, J.D. *Codes and Contradictions: Race, Gender Identity, and Schooling*. Albany: SUNY Press, 2000.

Weis, L. *Class Reunion: The Remaking of the American White Working Class*. New York: Routledge, 2004.

———. *Working Class without Work: High School Students in a Deindustrializing Economy*. New York: Routledge, 1990.

Weis, L., A. Proweller, and C. Centrie. "Excavating a 'Moment in History': Privilege and Loss inside White Working-Class Masculinity." In *Off White: Readings on Power, Privilege and Resistance*, edited by M. Fine, L. Weis, P. Pruitt and A. Burns. New York: Routledge, 2004.

Willis, P. *Learning to Labor: How Working Class Kids Get Working Class Jobs*. New York: Columbia University Press, 1977.

Zweig, M. *The Working Class Majority: America's Best Kept Secret*. Ithaca: Cornell University Press, 2000.

———, ed. *What's Class Got to Do with It? American Soceity in the Twenty-First Century*. Ithaca and London: ILR Press and imprint of Cornell University Press, 2004.

Index

About the Author

Carrie Freie is an assistant professor of education at Penn State Altoona where she teaches courses in educational theory and policy. She holds a master's degree in cultural anthropology from University at Albany, State University of New York and a PhD in Sociology of Education from University at Buffalo, the State University of New York. Her work combines anthropological and sociological methods toward the study of education. She has published work in *Play and Culture Studies*, *The Social Studies* and the second edition of *Invisible Children in Society and Its Schools*.